The Inflation Beater's Investment Guide

ALSO BY THE AUTHOR

A Random Walk Down Wall Street

The Inflation Beater's Investment Guide

ALSO BY THE AUTHOR

A Random Walk Down Wall Street

THE INFLATION BEATER'S INVESTMENT GUIDE

Winning Strategies for the 1980s

BURTON G. MALKIEL

W·W·NORTON & COMPANY · New York · London

For
FRICKA

Copyright © 1980 by Burton G. Malkiel
Published simultaneously in Canada by George J. McLeod Limited, Toronto.
Printed in the United States of America.

All Rights Reserved

First Edition

LIBRARY OF CONGRESS CATALOGING IN PUBLICATION DATA

Malkiel, Burton Gordon.
The inflation beater's investment guide.

Includes index.
1. Investments—Handbooks, manuals, etc. 2. Inflation (Finance)—Handbooks, manuals, etc. I. Title.
HG4521.M283 1980   332.6'78   80-10874
ISBN 0 393 01355 3

1 2 3 4 5 6 7 8 9 0

4

Contents

Preface and Acknowledgments

Academics love to communicate. Some even like to practice what they preach. I do my practicing by sitting on the investment committees for some large institutional investors controlling tens of billions of dollars of assets. My preaching, I found, was often restricted to my peers. I think it is important and useful, however, for academics also to write for a broader audience, particularly on subjects of interest to the general public. This helps shorten the lag between academic discovery and practical application. I have so thoroughly enjoyed my own forays into this arena that I have been persuaded to do so again.

In 1973 I wrote *A Random Walk Down Wall Street*, which was largely devoted to an exposition of academic research on the stock market. The focus of the present book is different: this book is primarily an investment guide to tell nonprofessionals how to handle their money in an era of inflation. It is a subject where the combination of practical experience and academic expertise can most helpfully be combined.

9

At the start of the book, I do pick up some of the themes from *Random Walk,* since I think they are essential for individuals who wish to make sensible decisions in financial markets. My aim is to provide only a brief updated review, with emphasis on knowledge we have accumulated during the 1970s. The major part of the book, however, is devoted to a practical, step-by-step investment guide to help overcome inflation. My thesis is that common stocks, which have been among the worse habitats for your money during the 1970s, are today both the best value and the most dependable inflation hedge available. I then give specific advice on how to build a stock portfolio, including how to buy premium stocks at substantial discounts. The book is designed to be as comprehensive as it is practical to help investors gear all their investments to inflation. I cover the gamut of investments from liquid asset funds and floating-rate notes to real estate and gold.

My debts of gratitude to people and institutions who have assisted me are enormous. I have received unusually helpful comments on drafts of this manuscript from Jeffrey Balash, Peter Bernstein, John Bogle, Paul Firstenberg, William Freund, and William McCleery. John Bogle also furnished me with statistical materials that were exceedingly useful in the preparation of some of the tables. It is particularly appropriate, however, that I emphasize the usual *caveat* that the above-named individuals are blameless for any errors of fact or judgment in these pages.

I have been extremely fortunate to have the services of Deborah Bickelman as my research assistant during the preparation of the book. She has been invaluable in ferreting out information, preparing exhibits, and checking data. Equally important has been the assistance of my secretary, Barbara Grindle, who not only faithfully typed and kept track of various drafts of the manuscript, but also did a good deal of data gathering and fact checking. Phyllis Durepos and Louise Olson pitched in by accurately typing many of the final drafts of the chapters. James Rauch offered extremely valuable research assistance and Elvira Krespach provided most helpful computer programming. I also want to thank Phyllis Byrd and Cathy James, who were helpful in many ways.

A vital contribution was made by Patricia Taylor, a professional writer and editor who worked with me on *Random Walk*. Once again, she read through two complete drafts of the book and made innumerable contributions to the style, organization, and content of the manuscript. She deserves much of the credit for whatever lucid writing can be found in these pages.

The individuals who have influenced me and have thereby contributed to this book are far too numerous to mention. I must at the very least, however, take note of the contributions of Alan Abelson, Edgar Bunce, Don Conlan, Frank Hoenemeyer, Robert Kirby, Alan Greenspan, Douglas Love, Andrew Tobias, and Edward Zinbarg.

Much of the research underlying the recommendations in this book was done at Princeton University's Financial Research Center, which in turn has been generously supported by the Charles E. Merrill Trust and the John Weinberg Foundation.

My association with W. W. Norton & Company continues to be a pleasant one, and I am particularly grateful to Starling Lawrence, Donald Lamm, and Robert Kehoe for their help and encouragement. Finally, I am enormously grateful to my wife and to my son, whose patience and understanding have made this book possible.

I mentioned at the outset that I have benefited in writing this book from my professional association with several financial institutions. One of these associations, my membership on the Board Directors of the Vanguard Group of Investment Companies, presents at least the appearance of a conflict of interest, however. Since Vanguard is one of the largest investment company complexes, and since a part of the overall investment strategy I recommend involves the purchase of investment company shares, I do mention some of the Vanguard funds by name in this book, along with the names of many other funds. I believe the best way to deal with the appearance of a problem is to make a full disclosure of my association, as I do here and as I will repeat at any mention of a fund with which I have any association.

BURTON G. MALKIEL

Princeton University
January 1980

The
Inflation
Beater's
Investment
Guide

CHAPTER 1

The Practical Lessons
of History for Investors

This book presents a succinct investment guide for the 1980s, covering everything from insurance to income taxes. It recognizes that the inflation rate in the 1980s is likely to be well above that of the past, and shows you how to manage your money so as better to cope with its ravages. It tells you how to save on taxes, buy life insurance, own your own home, avoid getting ripped off by banks and brokers, and even what to do about gold and diamonds. But primarily it is a book about common stocks. Contrary to popular opinion, I believe that at the start of the eighties they represent a unique investment opportunity, one which will provide generous returns and the best inflation hedge available.

Most investors establish their strategies by looking into a rearview mirror. What they see is that common stocks have provided lackluster returns for more than a decade. One backward-looking business magazine even thought it saw "The Death of Equities." Individual investors have been getting out of the market in record numbers, just as they rushed like lemmings to buy when past returns had been enormous. In my view this strategy is 100 percent wrong. Investors should be asking "What is going to be the best investment over the eighties?"—not "What investment was best in the seventies?" The same circumstances that depressed stock prices have now created the buying opportunity of a lifetime. And the conditions that made gold shine so brilliantly in the 1970s have now created enormous risks for gold investors.

I cannot convince you of the merit of common stocks and the myth of gold without some background on how assets are valued. Thus, the first two chapters are devoted largely to a description of both the principles and the history of investment valuations. They are, I believe, required reading for everyone who invests. They are written so that a person with no financial background at all can easily grasp the investment principles involved. Chapter 3 presents ten investment commandments for coping with inflation. It covers the gamut of individual financial needs from checking accounts to advice on whether to rent or buy a home. Chapter 4 argues the thesis of the book, that common stocks are an inflation hedge and should be the cornerstone of everyone's investment portfolio. Chapter 5 presents a practical, tested, and step-by-step guide to show how you can actually achieve rates of return from common stocks that will exceed those earned by the experts.

Inflation as a Fact of Life

In *A Random Walk Down Wall Street* I mentioned a handy rule to determine how long it would take to double dividends. Called the "Rule of 72," you simply divide a company's growth rate into the number 72 to find the number of years in which dividends would double. For example, when IBM's dividends were growing at a 15-percent rate, it took only five years (72 ÷ 15) for the dividend to double. Now, unfortunately, there seems to be a more macabre use for the Rule of 72. You divide the inflation rate into 72 to find out how long it will take your dollar to be worth half its present value in real purchasing power. If inflation were to continue at its 1979 double-digit (13-percent) rate, it would take only five and one-half years for your dollar to be worth fifty cents. This is a staggering thought to any retired person living on a fixed income.

It is important to realize that even a mild inflation can do plenty of damage. Even if we brought the inflation rate down to just over 5 percent—a target many economists might well describe as ridiculously optimistic—the effect on our purchasing power is still devastating. Table 1 shows what an average 5-percent inflation has done over the past eighteen years. My morning newspaper has risen 400 percent. So has my afternoon Hershey bar, and it's actually smaller than it was in 1962 when I was in graduate school. If inflation continues at its present rate, today's Hershey bar will cost seventy cents in 1990. It is clear that if we are to cope with even a mild inflation, we must undertake investment strategies that maintain our real purchasing power or we are doomed to an ever-decreasing standard of living.

TABLE 1

The Bite of Inflation

	Average 1962	Start 1980	Percentage increase	Compound annual rate of inflation (%)
Consumer Price Index	90.6	230	154	5.4
Hershey bar	$.05	$.25	400	9.4
New York Times	.05	.25	400	9.4
First-class Postage	.04	.15	275	7.7
Gasoline (gallon)	.31	1.15	271	7.6
Hamburger (McDonald's double)	.28[a]	.80	186	6.2
Chevrolet (Impala)	2529.00	6602.00	161	5.6
Refrigerator-freezer	470.00	530.00	13	0.7

SOURCE: *Forbes*, Nov. 1, 1977, for 1962 prices, and various government and private sources for current prices.
[a]1963 data.

Investing as a Way of Life Today

At this point, it's probably a good idea to explain what I mean by "investing" and how I distinguish this activity from "speculating." I view investing as a method of purchasing assets in order to gain profit in the form of reasonably predictable income (dividends, interest, or rentals) and/or appreciation *over the long term*. It is in the definition of the time period for the investment return and in the predictability of the returns that we can often distinguish an investment from a speculation. Having seen the movie *Superman* several times with my son Jonathan, an analogy comes to mind. When the evil Lothar bought land in Arizona with the idea that California would soon slide into the ocean, thereby quickly producing far more valuable beachfront property, he was speculating. Had he bought such land as a long-term holding after examining migration patterns, housing construction trends, and the availability of water supplies, he would probably be viewed as investing—particularly if he viewed the purchase as likely to produce a dependable future stream of cash returns.

Let me make it quite clear that this is not a book for speculators: I am not going to promise you overnight riches. Indeed, a subtitle for this book might well have been "The Get Rich Slowly But Surely Book." My defense of equities rests largely on the case that, at present prices, their stream of future dividend payments will produce excellent percentage returns in the decade ahead. Remember that with inflation as a fact of life, profitable investing as a way of life today means that you probably must obtain yearly returns of around 10 percent after taxes just to stay even. I am going to suggest particular investments that will bring you returns of 15 percent and more so that you should be ahead of the game.

Investing requires a lot of work, make no mistake about it. Romantic novels are replete with tales of great family fortunes lost through neglect or lack of knowledge on how to care for money. Who can forget the sounds of the cherry orchard being torn down in Chekov's great play. Free enterprise, not the Marxist system, caused the downfall of Chekov's family: they had not worked to keep their money. Even if you trust all your funds to an investment advisor or to a mutual fund, you still have to know which advisor or which fund is most suitable to handle your money. Armed with the information contained in this book, you should find it a bit easier to make your investment decisions.

Most important of all, however, is the fact that investing is *fun.* It's fun to put your intellect against that of the vast investment community and to find yourself rewarded with an increase in assets. It's exciting to review your investment returns and to see how they are accumulating at a faster rate than your salary. And it's also stimulating to learn about new ideas for products and services, and innovations in the forms of financial investments. A successful investor is generally a well-rounded individual who puts a natural curiosity and an intellectual interest to work to earn more money.

Investing in Theory

All investment returns—whether from common stocks or exceptional diamonds—are dependent, to varying degrees, on future events. That's what makes the fascination of investing: it's a gamble whose success depends on an ability to predict the future. Generally the pros use one of two approaches to asset valuation. I call one the "firm-foundation theory" and the other the "castle-in-the-air theory." Millions have been gained and lost on these theories. To add to the drama, they appear to be mutually exclusive. An understanding of these two approaches is essential to enable you to make sensible investment decisions. It is also a prerequisite for keeping you safe from serious blunders and for comprehending the specific investment strategy I will recommend later in the book.

The Firm-Foundation Theory

The firm-foundation theory argues that each investment instrument, be it a common stock or a piece of real estate, has a firm anchor of something called intrinsic value, which can be determined by careful analysis of present conditions and future prospects. When market prices fall below (rise above) this firm foundation of intrinsic value, a buying (selling) opportunity arises because this fluctuation will eventually be corrected—or so the theory goes. Investing then becomes a dull but straightforward matter of comparing something's actual price with its firm foundation of value.

Firm-foundation theorists view the worth of any investment as the present value of all future dollar benefits. The word "present" indicates that a distinction must be made between dollars expected immediately and those anticipated later on, which must be "discounted." All future income is worth less than money in hand, for if you had the money now you could be earning interest on it. In a very real sense, time is money.

The logic of the firm-foundation theory is quite respectable and can be illustrated best with common stocks. The theory stresses that a stock's value ought to consist of the stream of earnings a firm will be able to distribute in the future in the form of dividends. It stands to reason that the greater the present dividends and their rate of increase, the greater the value of the company. Thus, differences in growth rates are a major factor in stock valuation. And now the slippery little factor of future expectations sneaks in. Security analysts must estimate not only long-term growth rates but also how long an extraordinary growth can be maintained. When the market gets overly enthusiastic about how far in the future growth can continue, it is popularly held on Wall Street that "stocks are discounting not only the future but perhaps even the hereafter." The point is that the firm-foundation theory relies on some tricky forecasts of the extent and duration of future growth. The foundation of intrinsic value may thus be a less dependable one than is claimed.

While the anchor may be on the lightweight side, a major study by Princeton's Financial Research Center indicates that the firm-foundation theory is a major factor in stock valuation. The study focused on price/earnings (P/E) multiples rather than on the market prices themselves. This provides a good yardstick for comparing stocks—which have different prices and earnings—against one another. A stock selling at $100 per share with earnings of $10 per share would have the same P/E ratio (10) as a stock selling at $40 with earnings of $4 per share. It is the P/E multiple, not the dollar price, that really tells you how a stock is valued in the market.

It was easy to collect the first half of the data required. P/E multiples are printed daily in papers such as the *New York Times* and the *Wall Street Journal.* To obtain information on expected long-term growth rates, the Center surveyed several leading investment firms whose business it is to produce the forecasts upon which buy and sell recommendations are made. (I'll describe later how they make these forecasts.) Estimates were obtained from each firm of the five-year growth rates anticipated for a large sample of stocks. Results for a few representative securities are illustrated in Figure 1. It is clear that high P/E ratios are associated with high expected growth rates. This general pattern has held up in every year since 1961, when the Center began its study. There does seem to be a logic to market valuations.

In addition to demonstrating how the market values different growth rates, Figure 1 can also be used as a practical investment guide. Suppose you were considering the purchase of a stock with an anticipated 10-percent growth rate and you knew that, on average, stocks with 10-percent growth sold, like IBM, at 12 times earnings. If the stock you were considering sold at a price/earnings multiple of 20, you might reject the idea of buying the stock in favor of one more reasonably priced in terms of current market norms. If, on the other hand, your stock sold at a multiple below the average in the market for that growth rate, the security is said to represent a good value.

So far, so good. But our anchor runs into stormy seas with the specific premium the market puts on expected growth. It is always true that the market values growth, and that higher growth rates and larger multiples go hand in hand. But the crucial question is: How much more should you pay for higher growth? There is no consistent answer. In some periods, as in the early 1960s and early 1970s, when growth was thought to be especially

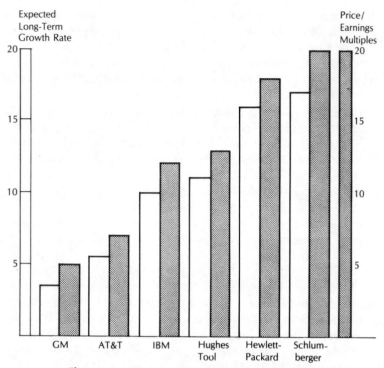

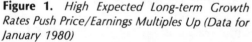

Figure 1. *High Expected Long-term Growth Rates Push Price/Earnings Multiples Up (Data for January 1980)*

desirable and stock market investors tended to be quite optimistic, the market paid an enormous price for stocks exhibiting high growth rates. At other times, such as the end of the 1970s and start of the 1980s, when investors were extremely wary of the stock market, high-growth stocks commanded only a modest premium over the multiples of common stocks in general. IBM is a good case in point. In 1972, IBM's long-term growth rate was estimated at 12.5 percent and its P/E was 40. In 1979, IBM's long-term growth estimate had slipped only slightly to 10.5 percent while its P/E ratio sank to 12. Today the P/E ratio for the major growth stocks averages only 10–20 percent above that for the market as a whole.

From a practical standpoint, the rapid changes in market valuations suggest that it would be very dangerous to use any one year's estimates as an indication of market norms. However, by comparing how growth stocks are currently valued with historical precedent, investors should at least be able to isolate those periods when stocks with good growth prospects seem to be quite richly priced in the market. I will return to this point in Chapter 5 and show how an understanding of these relationships may alert you to profitable buying opportunities and protect you from some of the madness that is sometimes associated with stock market prices.

The Castle-in-the-Air Theory

The castle-in-the-air theory of investing has nothing to do with intrinsic values. It concentrates on psychic values. Lord Keynes, a famous economist and outstandingly successful investor, enunciated the theory most lucidly in 1936. It was his opinion that professional investors prefer to devote their energies not to estimating intrinsic values, but rather to an analysis of how the crowd of investors is likely to behave in the future and how during periods of optimism they tend to build their hopes into castles in the air. The successful investor tries to beat the gun by estimating what investment situations are most susceptible to public castle-building and then buying before the crowd.

According to Keynes, the firm-foundation theory involved too much work and was of doubtful value. Keynes practiced what he preached. While London's financial men toiled many weary hours in darkened rooms, he played the market from his bed for half an hour each morning. This leisurely method of investing earned him several million pounds for his account and a tenfold increase in the market value of the endowment of his college, King's College, Cambridge.

With regard to stocks, Keynes noted that no one knows for sure what will influence future earnings prospects and dividend payments. As a result, Keynes said, most persons are "largely concerned, not with making superior long-term forecasts of the probable yield of an investment over its whole life, but with foreseeing changes in the conventional basis of valuation a short time ahead of the general public." Keynes, in other words, applied psychological principles rather than financial evaluation to the study of the stock market. He wrote, "It is not sensible to pay 25 for an investment of which you believe the prospective yield to justify a value of 30, if you also believe that the market will value it at 20 three months hence."

Keynes describes the playing of the stock market in terms readily understandable to his fellow Englishmen: it is analogous to entering a newspaper beauty-judging contest in which you have to select the six prettiest faces out of a hundred photographs. The prize goes to the person whose selections most nearly conform to those of the group as a whole.

The smart player recognizes that personal criteria of beauty are irrelevant in determining the contest winner. A better strategy is to select those faces the other players are likely to fancy. This logic tends to snowball. After all, the other contestants are likely to play the game with at least as keen a perception. Thus, the optimal strategy is not to pick those faces the player thinks are prettiest, nor those the other players are likely to fancy, but rather to predict what the average opinion is likely to think the average opinion will be, or to proceed even further along this sequence. So much for British beauty contests.

The newspaper-contest analogy represents the ultimate form of a castle-in-the-air theory of price determination. An investment is worth one price to a buyer because he expects to sell it to someone else at a higher price. The investment, in other words, holds itself up by its own bootstraps. The new buyer in turn anticipates that future buyers will assign a still higher value.

In this kind of world, there is a sucker born every minute—and he exists to buy your investments at a higher price than you paid for them. Any price will do as long as others may be willing to pay more. There is no reason, only mass psychology. All the smart investor has to do is to beat the gun—get in at the very beginning. This theory might less charitably be called the "greater fool theory." It's perfectly all right to pay three times what something is worth as long as later on you can find some innocent to pay five times what it's worth.

Investing in Practice

To paraphrase Shakespeare slightly, theories are but dreams till their effects be tried. Has investing over the centuries reflected the two theories just described?

The Madness of Crowds

History provides many illustrations of market participants throwing over firm foundations of value for the dubious but thrilling assumption that they can make a killing by building castles in the air. The castles that have been built have been based on such things as tulip bulbs, real estate, and common stocks.

History, in this instance, does teach a lesson: while the castle-in-the-air theory can well explain such speculative binges, outguessing the reactions of a fickle crowd is a most dangerous game. It is a lesson that needs to be cried out. Skyrocketing markets that depend on purely psychic support have invariably succumbed to the financial laws of gravity. Unsustainable prices may persist for years, but eventually they reverse themselves. Such reversals come with the suddenness of an earthquake; and the bigger the binge, the greater the resulting hangover. Few of the reckless builders of castles in the air have been nimble enough to anticipate these reversals perfectly and escape without losing a great deal of money when everything came tumbling down.

Tulip Bulbs. The tulip-bulb craze was one of the most spectacular get-rich-quick binges in history. Its excesses become even more vivid when one realizes that it happened in staid old Holland in the early seventeenth century. The events leading to this speculative frenzy were set in motion in 1593 when a newly appointed botany professor from Vienna brought to Leyden a collection of unusual plants which had originated in Turkey. The Dutch were fascinated with this new addition to the garden—but not with the professor's asking price (he had hoped to sell the bulbs and make a handsome profit). One night a thief broke into the professor's house and stole the bulbs, which were subsequently sold at a lower price but at greater profit.

Over the next decade or so the tulip became a popular but expensive item in Dutch gardens. Many of these flowers succumbed to a nonfatal virus known as mosaic. It was this mosaic that helped to trigger the wild speculation in tulip bulbs. The mosaic caused the tulip petals to develop contrasting colored stripes, or "flames." The Dutch valued highly these infected bulbs, called "bizarres." In a short time, popular taste dictated that the more bizarre a bulb, the greater the cost of owning it.

Slowly, tulipmania set in. At first, bulb merchants simply tried to predict the most popular varigated style for the coming year, much as clothing manufacturers do in gauging the public's taste in fabric, color, and hemlines. Then they would buy an extra-large stockpile to anticipate a rise in price. Tulip-bulb prices began to rise wildly. The more expensive the bulbs became, the more people viewed them as smart investments. Charles Mackay, who chronicled these events in his book *Extraordinary Popular Delusions,* noted that the ordinary industry of the country was dropped in favor of speculation in tulip bulbs: "Nobles, citizens, farmers, mechanics, seamen, footmen, maid-servants, even chimney sweeps and old clotheswomen dabbled in tulips." Everyone imagined that the passion for tulips would last forever, and buyers from all over the world would come to Holland and pay whatever prices were asked for them.

Much like gold speculation today, people who said tulip prices could not possibly go higher watched with chagrin as their friends and relatives made enormous profits. It was hard not to resist; few Dutchmen did. In the last years of the tulip spree, which lasted approximately from 1634 to 1638, people started to barter even their personal belongings, such as land, jewels, and furniture, to obtain the bulbs that would make them even wealthier.

The history of the period was filled with many tragicomic episodes. For example, one incident concerned a returning sailor who brought news to a wealthy merchant of the arrival of a shipment of new goods. The merchant rewarded him with a breakfast of fine red herring. Seeing what he thought was an onion on the merchant's counter, and no doubt thinking it very much out of place amid silks and velvets, he proceeded to take it as a relish for his herring. Little did he dream that the "onion" would have fed a whole ship's crew for a year. It was a costly Semper Augustus tulip bulb. The sailor paid dearly for his relish —his no longer grateful host had him imprisoned for several months on a felony charge.

As happens in all speculative crazes, prices had been high for so long that some people decided they would be prudent and sell their bulbs. Soon others followed suit. Like a snowball rolling downhill, bulb deflation grew at an increasingly rapid pace and in no time at all panic reigned.

Government ministers stated officially that there was no reason for tulip bulbs to fall in price—but no one listened. Dealers went bankrupt and refused to honor their commitments to buy tulip bulbs. A government plan to settle all contracts at 10 percent of their face value was frustrated when bulbs fell even below this mark. And prices continued to decline. Down and down they went until the tulip bulb became almost worthless—selling for no more than the price of a common onion.

And what of those who had sold out early in the game? In the end, they too were engulfed by the tulip craze. For the final chapter of this bizarre story is that the shock generated by the boom and collapse led to a prolonged depression in Holland. No one was spared.

New Concepts and Issues. A century later, speculative frenzy reared its deadly head in England. The time was ripe for a new-issue craze. A long period of English prosperity had resulted in

fat savings and thin investment outlets. One of the first companies organized to capitalize on this situation was the South Sea
Company. In return for assuming £10 million of government
debt, the company was granted a monopoly on South Sea trade.
Rumors—aided, and indeed probably generated, by the company's directors—had it that the company would corner the trade
on Mexican gold. The price of the stock rose to dizzying heights
with no basis in actual performance results. At the same time, the
inflated total market value of the stock of the Mississippi Company in France was more than eighty times that of all the gold and
silver in the country.

Given the success of these companies, investors looked for
other new ventures where they could get in on the ground floor.
Just as speculators today search for the next Xerox and the next
IBM, so in England in the early 1800s they looked for the next
South Sea Company. Promoters obliged by organizing and
bringing to the market a flood of new issues to meet the insatiable
craving for investment.

The public, it seemed, would buy anything. They bought new
issues in nearly one hundred different projects. These companies
offered ventures ranging from the ingenious to the absurd—from
importing Spanish jackasses (although there was clearly an abundant supply of English jackasses) to making salt water fresh.
These companies received the name of "bubbles"—they were
easily popped.

My favorite bubble is that blown up by the unknown soul who
started "A Company for carrying on an undertaking of great
advantage, but nobody to know what it is." The prospectus promised unheard-of rewards. At nine o'clock in the morning, when
the subscription books opened, crowds of people from all walks
of life practically beat down the door in an effort to subscribe.
Within five hours a thousand investors handed over their money
for shares in the company. Not being greedy himself, the pro-
moter promptly closed up shop and set off for the continent. He
was never heard from again.

Not all investors in the bubble companies believed in the feasi-
bility of the schemes to which they subscribed. People were "too

sensible" for that. They did believe, however, in the "greater fool" theory—that prices would rise, that buyers would be found, and that they would make money. Thus, most investors considered their actions the height of rationality as, at least for a while, they could sell their shares at a premium in the "after market," that is, the trading market in the shares after their initial issue.

Many individual bubbles had been pricked without dampening the speculative enthusiasm, but the deluge came when the South Sea Company burst. Realizing that the price of the shares in the market bore no relationship to the real prospects of the company, the directors had sold out.

The news leaked and so did the stock. Soon the price of the shares collapsed and panic reigned. Government officials tried in vain to restore confidence and a complete collapse of the public credit was barely averted. Similarly, the price of the Mississippi Company fell to a pittance. Big losers in the South Sea bubble included Isaac Newton, who exclaimed, "I can calculate the motions of heavenly bodies, but not the madness of people."

To protect the public from further abuses, the British parliament passed a bill called the Bubble Act. It forbade the issuing of stock certificates by companies. For over a century, until 1825 when the act was repealed, there were relatively few share certificates in the British market.

Real Estate. In conquering an entire continent, it would appear only natural that Americans would succumb to a real estate boom. One of the greatest centered on Florida in the middle 1920s. The climate was just right. The population was steadily growing and housing was in short supply. Land values began increasing rapidly. Stories of investments doubling and tripling attracted speculators from all over the country. Easy credit terms added fuel to the speculative frenzy. "This market has no downside risk," the land speculators opined, as Dutchmen undoubtedly said to each other about the tulip-bulb market in an earlier time.

There are reports of Palm Beach land bought for $800,000 in 1923, subdivided and resold in 1924 for $1.5 million. By the following year the land sold at $4 million. At the top of the boom there were 75,000 real estate agents in Miami, one-third of the entire population of the city.

Inevitably the boom ended, as do all speculative crazes. By 1926 new buyers could no longer be found and prices softened. Then the speculators dumped their holdings on the market and a complete collapse ensued.

The Great Stock Crash. With this Florida experience so recently in mind one would have thought that investors would have avoided a similar misadventure on Wall Street. But Florida was only a regional prelude to what came next. Beginning in 1928, stock market speculation became a national pastime. It was central to our culture. John Brooks, in *Once in Golconda*, [1] recounted the remarks of a British correspondent newly arrived in New York: "You could talk about Prohibition, or Hemingway, or air conditioning, or music, or horses, but in the end you had to talk about the stock market, and that was when the conversation became serious." Borrowing to buy stocks (buying on margin) increased from only $1 billion in 1921 to almost $9 billion in 1929.

Unfortunately, there were hundreds of smiling operators only too glad to help the public construct castles in the air. Manipulation on the stock exchange set new records for unscrupulousness. Investment pools would create fictitious stock exchange activity to generate speculative enthusiasm for particular stocks. Tip-sheet writers and market commentators under the control of the pool manager would tell of exciting developments in the offing. Sometimes, corporate insiders helped the process along—ensuring a flow of increasingly favorable news from the company. If all went well, and in the speculative atmosphere of the 1928–29 period it could hardly miss, the combination of tape activity and managed news would bring the public in. One investment pool raised the price of RCA stock 61 points in four days.

Some idea of the extent of the speculative mania can be seen

---

[1]Golconda, now in ruins, was a city in India. According to legend, everyone who passed through it became rich.

by comparing the stock prices of some of the bluest blue-chip securities at the beginning of March 1928 (after several years of rising prices) with the prices at the start of September 1929. General Electric rose from 128¾ to 396¼, a gain of 208 percent in eighteen months. RCA did far better, rising from 94½ to 505, a gain of 434 percent. The sky seemed the limit as prices often rose 15 points a day.

To be sure, there were skeptics. Roger Babson, a frail, goateed, pixyish-looking financial adviser from Wellesley, Massachusetts, predicted that a crash was coming. But Babson had been predicting a crash for years and Wall Street professionals greeted these pronouncements from the "prophet of loss," as he was known, with their usual derision. Even "wise" academics disagreed with Babson. Professor Irving Fisher of Yale, one of the progenitors of the intrinsic-value theory, offered his soon-to-be-immortal opinion that stocks had reached what looked like a "permanently high plateau." Indeed, even when prices started down during September 1929, the indomitable Fisher dismissed the decline as a "shaking out of the lunatic fringe that attempts to speculate on margin." He went on to say that prices of stocks during the boom had not caught up with their real value and would go higher. Among other things, the professor believed that the market had not yet reflected the beneficent effects of Prohibition, which had made the American worker "more productive and dependable." President Hoover agreed. He said, "The fundamental business of the country . . . is on a sound and prosperous basis."

The crash occurred in October. On October 24, many stocks dropped $5 and $10 per share on each trade. Some issues dropped 40–50 points in a couple of hours. October 29 was the most catastrophic day in the history of the New York Stock Exchange. Prices fell almost perpendicularly. Between September and November, General Electric fell from 396¼ to 168⅛. RCA did even worse, falling to just over 25 percent of its early September value by mid-November 1929.

Perhaps the best summary of the debacle was given by *Variety*, the show-business weekly, which headlined the story "Wall Street Lays an Egg." The speculative boom was dead and billions of dollars of share values—as well as the dreams of millions—were wiped out. But the worst was yet to come. By 1932 GE sold at only 8½. RCA sold at 2½. The crash in the stock market was followed by the most devastating depression in the history of the country.

The Insanity of Institutions

There was a lesson in the great stock crash and it was that there is more to investing than just sheer speculation. Many people, however, thought the lesson was that the individual buyer should beware, that it was better to trust your money to a "pro," who knows what it's all about. So that's what happened. The growth of the money "pros" has been astounding. In 1960, institutions and other professional investors accounted for almost half the shares traded on the New York Stock Exchange; surveys in the late 1970s indicate that this figure may have increased to around 70 percent.

While the crowd may be mad, one would hope that the institution is above that. The hard-headed, sharp-penciled reasoning of the pros ought to guarantee that the extravagant excesses of the past will be avoided. Yet throughout the past twenty years of institutional domination of the market, prices often gyrated more rapidly and by much greater amounts than could plausibly be explained by apparent changes in their anticipated intrinsic values.

Of course, we should not generalize from an isolated instance. But professional investors did participate in at least three distinct speculative movements during the decades of the 1960s and 1970s. These events contain important lessons for investors and are described below.

Growth Stocks and New Issues. In the 1959–61 period, growth was a magic word. It was the corollary to the "Soaring Sixties," the wonderful decade to come. And hand in hand with growth were glamorous new technologies. Wall Street was eager to pay good money for space travel, transistors, Klystron tubes, optical

scanners, and other esoteric things. Backed by this strong enthusiasm, the price of securities in these businesses rose wildly.

By 1959 the traditional rule that stocks should sell at a multiple of 10–15 times their earnings has been supplanted by multiples of 50–100 times earnings for the most glamorous issues. For example, at the peak of the craze in 1961, Control Data, then a new computer company, sold for over 200 times its previous year's earnings, a price/earnings multiple that could not be justified on firm-foundation principles. But investors firmly believed that later in the wonderful decade of the sixties, buyers would eagerly come forward to pay even higher prices. Lord Keynes must have smiled quietly from wherever it is that economists go when they die.

I had just gone to work on Wall Street during the boom and recall vividly one of the senior partners of my firm shaking his head and admitting that he knew of no one over forty, with any recollection of the 1929–32 crash, who would buy and hold the high-priced growth stocks. But the young Turks held sway. The sky was the limit and the growth stocks were the ones that were going up. *Newsweek* quoted one broker as saying that speculators have the idea that anything they buy "will double overnight. The horrible thing is, it has happened."

Some people must have read their English history. To assuage the insatiable thirst of investors for the space-age stocks of the soaring sixties, promoters began to create new offerings by the dozens. (More were offered in this 1959–62 period than at any other time in history.) In place of bubbles, we now had "tronics," since the stock offerings often included some garbled version of the word "electronics" in their titles, even if the companies had nothing to do with the electronics industry. For example, American Music Guild, whose business consisted entirely of the door-to-door sale of phonograph records and players, changed its name to Space-Tone before "going public." The shares were sold to the public at 2, and within a few weeks rose to 14.

Jack Dreyfus, of Dreyfus and Company, commented on the mania as follows: "Take a company that's been making shoelaces for forty years and sells at a respectable six times earnings ratio.

Change the name from Shoelaces, Inc., to Electronics and Silicon Furth-Burners. In today's market, the words 'electronics' and 'silicon' are worth fifteen times earnings. However, the real play comes from the word 'furth-burners,' which no one understands. A word that no one understands entitles you to double your entire score. Therefore, we have six times earnings for the shoelace business and fifteen times earnings for electronics and silicon, or a total of twenty-one times earnings. Multiply this by two for furth-burners, and we now have a score of forty-two times earnings for the new company."

The "tronics" boom came back to earth in 1962. The tailspin started early in the year and exploded in a horrendous selling wave five months later. Yesterday's hot issue became today's cold turkey. The shares of most of the new issues of the early 1960s continued to fall until eventually they were almost worthless:

Performance and Concepts. Our next speculative mania came into being during the mid-sixties when there was heightened competition among mutual funds for the customer's dollar. Performance became the new golden calf. It meant that a fund performing better than the others (that is, the value of the stocks in its portfolio went up faster than the stocks in its competitors' portfolios) was a far easier fund to sell to the public than one with a less lustrous record. So, with the public buying, mutual fund salesmen began to clamor for even greater performance.

And perform the funds did—at least over short periods of time. Fred Carr's highly publicized Enterprise Fund racked up a 117-percent total return (including both dividends and capital gains) in 1967, and followed this with a 44-percent return in 1968. The corresponding figures for the Standard & Poor's 500 Stock Index were 25 percent and 11 percent, respectively. This performance brought large amounts of new money into the fund, and into other funds that could boast glamorous performances.

The performance game was not limited to mutual funds. It spread to all kinds of investing institutions. Businessmen who had to make constantly larger contributions to their workers' pension funds to meet retirement obligations began to ask pointedly whether they might be able to reduce their current expenses by switching more of the fund from fixed-income bonds into common stocks with exciting growth possibilities. Even university endowment-fund managers were pressured to strive for performance. McGeorge Bundy of the Ford Foundation chided the portfolio managers of universities:

It is far from clear that trustees have reason to be proud of their performance in making money for their colleges. We recognize the risks of unconventional investing, but the true test of performance in the handling of money is the record of achievement, not the opinion of the respectable. We have the preliminary impression that over the long run caution has cost our colleges and universities much more than imprudence or excessive risk-taking.

And so performance investing took hold of Wall Street in the late 1960s. The commandments for fund managers were simple: concentrate your holdings in a relatively few stocks. And because near-term performance was especially important (investment services began to publish weekly records of mutual fund performance), it would be best to buy stocks with an exciting concept and a compelling story. You had to be sure the market would recognize the beauty of your stock now—not far into the future. Hence, the birth of the so-called concept stock.

Xerox was a classic example. The concept was machines making dry copies by electrostatic transference. The company, Xerox, with its patent protection and its running head start, could look forward to several years of increased earnings. It was a true story, a believable story, one that would quicken the pulse of any good performance-fund manager. But even if the story were not totally believable, as long as the investment manager was convinced that the average opinion would think that the average opinion would believe the story, that's all that was needed. The "youthful gunslingers," as performance-fund managers were often called, had no use for standard security analysts who could tell you how many railroad ties Penn Central had but not when the company was about to go bankrupt. "I don't want to listen to that kind of security analyst," one of Wall Street's gunslingers told me. "I just want a good story or a good concept."

Eventually it reached a point where any concept would do. Enter Cortess W. Randell. His concept was a youth company for the youth market. He became founder, president, and major stockholder of National Student Marketing. Randell sold an image—one of affluence and success. He owned a personal white Lear Jet named *Snoopy,* an apartment in New York's Waldorf Towers, a $600,000 castle with a mock dungeon in Virginia, and a fifty-five-foot yacht that slept twelve. Randell's real métier was evangelism. When he told meetings of security analysts that NSM was well on its way toward becoming a $700-million marketing organization, they listened with faith, respect, and awe.

The concept that Wall Street bought from Randell was that a single company could specialize in servicing the needs of young people. Subsidiary companies sold magazine subscriptions, books and records, posters, paper dresses, guidebooks for summer jobs, student directories, a computer dating service, youth airfare cards, sweatshirts, live entertainment programs, and a variety of consumer staples. Each of the constituent companies had something to do with the college-age youth market. This was the age when no one over 30 was to be trusted. The youthful gunslingers loved the concept of a full-service company to exploit the youth subculture. Few bothered to take a look at the "creative" accounting practices that held up the concept, not even those trustworthy investment managers at Bankers Trust, Morgan Guaranty, and Boston's venerable State Street Fund. Pension funds, including General Mills, bought heavily; and United States Trust Company (the country's largest trust company) bought the stock for many of its accounts. University endowment-fund managers, heeding the words of McGeorge Bundy, also bought in the mad scramble for performance. Blocks of NSM were bought by Harvard, Cornell, and the University of Chicago. Bundy himself practiced what he preached, and the previously conservatively managed Ford Foundation Fund also bought a large block.

Other popular concepts were health care, environment, and

best of all, "performance" itself, as exemplified in that grand old company, Performance Systems (renamed from Minnie Pearl's Chickens). Table 2 shows the high prices and enormous price/ earnings multiples of stocks in these concept areas. The number of institutional holders (probably understated) for each security is also shown. Clearly, institutional investors are at least as adept as the general public at building castles in the air. The ∞ shown in the table under "price/earnings multiple" for Performance Systems indicates that the multiple was infinity. The company had no earnings at all to divide into the stock's price at the time it reached its high in 1968.

Why did the stocks actually perform so badly? One general answer was that their price/earnings multiples were inflated beyond reason. If a multiple of 100 drops to a more normal multiple

TABLE 2
The Decline of Concept Stocks

Security	High price 1968–69	Price/ earnings multiple at high	Number of institutional holders year-end 1969	Low price 1970	Percentage decline
Four Seasons Nursing Centers of America	90¾	113.4	24	0.20	99
National Environment Corp.	27	103.8	8	⅜	99
National Student Marketing	35¾ [a]	111.7	21	⅞	98
Performance Systems	23	∞	13	⅛	99

[a]Adjusted for subsequent stock split.

of 15, you have lost 85 percent of your investment right there. But in addition, most of the concept companies of the time ran into severe operating difficulties. These companies were run by men who were primarily promoters, not sharp-penciled operating managers. In addition, fraudulent practices were common. For example, Performance Systems reported profits of $3.2 million in 1969. The SEC claimed that this report was "false and misleading." In 1972 Performance Systems issued a revision of the 1969 report. Apparently a loss of $1.3 million more accurately reflected 1969 operations.

And so when the 1969–71 bear market came, these concept stocks went down just as fast as they went up. In the end it was the pros who were conned most of all. While there is nothing wrong with seeking good performance, the mad rush to outgun the competition week by week had disastrous consequences. The cult of performance and the concept of "concept" stocks were henceforth greeted with disdain when mentioned in Wall Street.

The Nifty Fifty. Like general's fighting the last war, Wall Street's pros were not planning to repeat the mistakes of the 1960s in the 1970s. No more would they buy small electronics companies or exciting concept stocks. Reason had returned and with it a return to "sound principles" that translated to investing in blue-chip companies with proven growth records. These were companies, so the thinking went, that would never come crashing down like the speculative favorites of the 1960s. Nothing could be more prudent than to buy their shares and then relax on the golf course while the long-term rewards materialized.

There were only four dozen or so of these premier growth stocks that so fascinated the institutional investors. The names were very familiar—IBM, Xerox, Avon Products, Kodak, McDonald's, Polaroid, and Disney, to list a few. They were called the Nifty Fifty. They were "big capitalization" stocks, which meant that an institution could buy a good-sized position without disturbing the market. And since most pros realized that picking the exact correct time to buy is difficult if not impossible, these stocks seemed to make a great deal of sense. So what if you paid a price that was temporarily too high? Since these stocks were proven growers, sooner or later the price you paid would be justified. In addition, these were stocks—like the family heirlooms—you would never sell. Hence these stocks were also called "one-decision" stocks. You made a decision to buy them once and then your portfolio management problems were over.

These stocks provided security blankets for institutional investors in another way too. They were so respectable. Your colleagues could never question your prudence in investing in IBM. True, you could lose money if IBM went down, but that was not considered imprudent (as it would be to lose money in a Performance Systems or a National Student Marketing). Like greyhounds in chase of the mechanical rabbit, big pension funds, insurance companies, and bank trust funds loaded up on the Nifty Fifty one-decision growth stocks. Hard as it is to believe, the institutions had actually started to speculate in blue chips. This is a case of classic insanity. The heights to which the stocks rose were unbelievable. In Table 3 I have listed the price/earnings ratios achieved by a handful of these stocks in 1972. For comparison, the earnings multiples as of the start of the 1980s are listed too. Institutional managers blithely ignored the fact that no sizable

TABLE 3
P/Es of Some of the Nifty Fifty

Security	Price/earnings multiple 1972	Price/earnings multiple 1980
Sony	92	17
Polaroid	90	16
McDonald's	83	9
Intl. Flavors	81	12
Walt Disney	76	11
Hewlett-Packard	65	18

company could ever grow fast enough to justify an earnings multiple of 80 or 90. They once again proved the maxim that stupidity well packaged can sound like wisdom.

Perhaps one might argue that the craze was simply a manifestation of the return of confidence in late 1972. Richard Nixon had been reelected by a landslide, peace was "at hand" in Vietnam, price controls were due to come off, inflation was apparently "under control," and no one knew what OPEC was. But in fact when the market started to decline in early 1972, the Nifty Fifty mania became even more pathological. For as the market in general collapsed, the Nifty Fifty continued to command record earnings multiples and, on a relative basis, the overpricing greatly increased. There appeared to be a "two-tier" market. *Forbes* magazine commented as follows:

[The Nifty Fifty appeared to rise up] from the ocean; it was as though all of the U.S. but Nebraska had sunk into the sea. The two tier market really consisted of one tier and a lot of rubble down below.

What held the Nifty Fifty up? The same thing that held up tulip-bulb prices in long-ago Holland—popular delusions and the madness of crowds. The delusion was that these companies were so good that it didn't matter what you paid for them; their inexorable growth would bail you out.

The end was inevitable. The Nifty Fifty craze ended like all other speculative manias. The Nifty Fifty were—in the words of *Forbes* columnist Martin Sosnoff—taken out and shot one by one. The oil embargo hit Disney and its large stake in Disneyland and Disneyworld. Production problems with new cameras hit Polaroid. The stocks sank like stones into the ocean. A critical cover story in widely respected *Forbes* magazine sent Avon Products down almost 50 percent in six months. The real problem was never the particular needle that pricked each individual bubble. The problem was that the stocks were simply ridiculously overpriced. Sooner or later the same money managers who worshiped the Nifty Fifty decided to make a second decision and sell. In the debacle that followed, the premier growth stocks fell completely from favor and remain so today at the start of the 1980s. Again the lessons of market history are clear. It is very difficult to be neutral about things so difficult to forecast as the future earnings prospects of corporations (or other investors' hopes and fears). Moreover, there are styles and fashions in investors' evaluations of securities. As I shall indicate in Chapter 5, this extreme overreaction to growth stocks following the collapse of the Nifty Fifty in the 1970s has created excellent opportunities for investors in the 1980s.

The Practical Theories for Investors

This chapter began with a description of the firm-foundation theory of stock values which indicated that "fundamental" considerations such as earnings growth do influence the prices of common stocks. There is a yardstick for value, but we have seen that it is a most flexible and undependable instrument. To change the metaphor, stock prices are in a sense anchored to certain "fundamentals" but the anchor is easily pulled up and then dropped in another place. For the standards of value, we have found, are not the fixed and immutable standards that characterize the laws of physics, but rather the more flexible and fickle relationships that are consistent with a marketplace heavily influenced by mass psychology.

Not only does the market change the values it puts on the various fundamental determinants of stock prices, but the most important of these fundamentals are themselves liable to change depending on the state of market psychology. Stocks are bought on expectations—not on facts. Future earnings growth is not easily estimated, even by market professionals. In times of great optimism it is very easy for investors to convince themselves that their favorite corporations can enjoy substantial and persistent growth over an extended period of time. By raising his estimates of growth, even the most sober firm-foundation theorist can convince himself to pay any price whatever for a share.

During periods of extreme pessimism, many security analysts

will not project any growth that is not "visible" to them over the very short run and hence will estimate only the most modest of growth rates for the corporations they follow. But if expected growth rates themselves and the price the market is willing to pay for this growth can both change rapidly on the basis of market psychology, then it is clear that the concept of a *firm* intrinsic value for shares must be an elusive will-o'-the-wisp. As an old Wall Street proverb runs: No price is too high for a bull or too low for a bear.

Dreams of castles in the air, of getting rich quick, do play a role —at times a dominant one—in determining actual stock prices. In this chapter I have documented several examples from both the distant and the recent past. Why are memories so short? Why do speculative crazes seem so isolated from the lessons of history? I have no apt answer to offer, but I am convinced that Bernard Baruch was correct in suggesting that a study of these events can help equip investors for survival. The consistent losers in the market, from my personal experience, are those who are unable to resist being swept up in some kind of tulip-bulb craze. It is not hard, really, to make money in the market. What is hard is to avoid the alluring temptation to throw money away on short, get-rich-quick speculative binges.

And yet the melody lingers on. While common stocks are virtually ignored, gold has recently been advancing toward $1000 an ounce. At the end of the 1970s, eager real estate speculators in places like California were turning properties around with profits of 25 percent in a matter of days. The notion is always the same: there will always be some greater fool to pay an even greater price. Will the music stop again?

Markets, whether for common stocks, real properties, or precious metals, will not be a perpetual tulip-bulb craze. The existence of some generally accepted principles of valuation does serve as a kind of balance wheel. For the castle-in-the-air investor might well consider that if prices get too far out of line with normal valuation standards, the average opinion may soon expect that others will anticipate a reaction. There is, after all, a firm foundation of value, albeit a very loose and flexible one. Sooner or later, however, all skyrocketing investments must measure up to this basic foundation of value. The ability to avoid being swept up in some frenzy of speculative enthusiasm is probably the most important factor in preserving the real value of one's capital and allowing it to grow. The lesson is so obvious and yet so easy to ignore.

CHAPTER **2**

The New
Investment Technology

In 1973, I published *A Random Walk Down Wall Street,* a book whose theses have become the core of what is now popularly called "The Efficient-Market Theory" or "The New Investment Technology." That book suggested that a blindfolded chimpanzee throwing darts at the *Wall Street Journal* could pick a portfolio of stocks that would perform as well as those carefully selected by the highest priced security analysts. Investment professionals as a group were portrayed as no better at managing a portfolio than a passive investor who just bought shares in the popular broad-based stock indexes and just held tight. Consistently superior skill in selecting stocks that have been under- or overvalued in the market is likely to be a very rare art. I presented evidence that over the long run investment returns are likely to be related to the risk assumed.

It was hard for people to be lukewarm about the book. People either loved it or hated it. *Forbes* commented, "Not more than half a dozen really good books have been written about investing in the past 50 years. This one may well belong in the classics category." The *Business Week* review, written by a leading Wall Street chartist, characterized the book as a disaster. The review was entitled "Down a blind alley with a random walker." A leading investment advisor ran a half-page ad in the *New York Times* railing against the efficient-market thesis. The ad was entitled "The greater fool theory: Summa cum laude from Princeton." In 1979, a game manufacturer, appropriately called Seat-of-the-Pants Management, Inc., marketed a portfolio selection game that consisted of a dart board printed with the daily stock charts and a set of so-called adviser darts.

One of the questions I am most frequently asked now is whether I still believe in the thesis expounded in *Random Walk*. The answer is a very clear yes. While there may well be exceptions to the thesis, as I freely admitted in 1973, by and large the evidence of recent history has been kind to the random walkers. Table 4 makes the case as well as any. In the five years following the publication of *Random Walk,* over three-quarters of the professionals who manage pension fund common stock portfolios were outperformed by the unmanaged Standard & Poor's Index. It is very clear that the "new view" of stock pricing, spawned by computer technology and reared by academic and business researchers, is one that deserves the attention of all investors.

In this chapter, I will briefly summarize the main tenets of the new investment technology and the evidence supporting it, especially as it has accumulated in recent years. My aim is not a

TABLE 4
Pension Funds Outperformed by S&P 500 Index

Time period	Percentage of pension funds outperformed by S&P 500 Index
5 years 1974–78	76
10 years 1969–78	84

complete exposition—a fuller story can be found in *Random Walk* —but rather to cover only the things you need to know in order to make intelligent investment decisions for the 1980s.

Traditional Techniques of Stock Market Analysis

The basic idea of the new investment technology is that securities markets are very efficient in digesting information. When information arises about a stock or about the future of the market in general, the news spreads very quickly and is quickly impounded into the price of securities. Thus, it is useless to try to use either technical analysis (an analysis of past price patterns in an attempt to divine the future) or fundamental analysis (an analysis of a particular company's earnings, its future prospects, etc., to determine a stock's proper value) to attempt to beat the market.

Technical Analysis

Technical analysis is essentially the construction and interpretation of stock charts. It involves a study of the past movements of both common stock prices and the volume of trading for a clue to the direction of future change. Its practitioners used to be called chartists, but that term is not too glamorous in today's sophisticated society, so now most of them go by the name of technicians. They believe that history is doomed to repeat itself. Once the pattern of stock market history reveals itself—and today a lot of expensive computer time is used to draw the picture— the technicians can then determine the market's future direction.

Most technicians do not even want to hear any information concerning the fundamental valuation factors that are of such concern to ordinary security analysts. A chart showing these prices and the volume of trading already comprises all the fundamental information, good or bad, that the security analyst can hope to know. The technician doesn't even care to know what business or industry the company is in. An uptrend formation in Tandem Computers has the same significance as the same formation in International Business Machines. One of the most prominent technicians, John Magee, operates from a small office in Springfield, Massachusetts, where even the windows are boarded up to prevent any outside influences from distracting his analysis.

The technician's basic thesis is that prices tend to move in trends. He believes that Newtonian principles apply to the stock market as well as to falling apples. A stock that is rising tends to keep on rising, whereas a stock at rest tends to remain at rest. The alleged persistence of trends in the market might occur for either of two reasons: first, it has been argued that the crowd instinct of mass psychology makes it so. When investors see the price of, say, Resorts International common going higher and higher, they want to jump on the bandwagon and join the rise. Indeed, the price rise itself helps fuel the enthusiasm in a self-fulfilling prophecy. Each rise in price just whets the appetite and makes investors expect a further rise. The same kind of scenario can be sketched out for a falling market as well. As you can see, this argument is consistent with the castle-in-the-air theory of stock pricing.

The second rationale concerns the unequal access to fundamental information about a company. When some favorable piece of news occurs, such as the discovery of a rich oil deposit, it is alleged that the geologist who found the deposit first buys the stock and causes its price to rise. The geologist then tells his friends, who proceed to buy. Then the geologist might tell the company management and these insiders next buy. Eventually, it is alleged, the professional investors find out and the big institutions put blocks of the shares in their portfolios. Finally, the poor slobs like you and me get the information and we buy, pushing the price still higher. This process is supposed to result in a rather gradual increase in the price of the stock when the news is good and a gradual decrease when the news is bad. The technicians claim that even if they do not have access to this inside information, observation of the price movements enables them to pick up the scent of the "smart money," and permits them to get in long before the general public. Most popular investment nostrums offered by brokers really rest on technical analysis. You may have heard a broker say, "Hold the winners, sell the losers"; "Buy strong stocks"; "Avoid this stock, it's acting poorly"; or "Don't fight the tape." All assume that trends will continue—they all rest on technical analysis.

Fundamental Analysis

This approach to the stock market shuns the esoteric trappings of technical analysis. Fundamental analysis deals with nuts and bolts. Most professional security analysts utilize this kind of analysis to determine a security's firm foundation of "value" or intrinsic worth. The most important component of this analysis is the estimation of the future stream of earnings and dividends for any company. In a sense, the fundamentalist is forward looking while the technician is backward looking. The fundamentalist not only looks at the past record of the company, but also analyzes the company's investment plans and budgets for the future, visits and appraises the company's management team (and sometimes even its nuts and bolts). The security analyst need not rely on the company's word that it has a successful casino in Atlantic City; he can visit the gaming tables himself. This process yields a wealth of data. The analyst must then separate the important from the unimportant facts. As Benjamin Graham put it in *The Intelligent Investor,* "Sometimes he reminds us a bit of the erudite major general in 'The Pirates of Penzance,' with his 'many cheerful facts about the square of the hypotenuse.' "

The final result of all this effort is to come up with a prediction of future earnings growth. Then the analyst applies the principles of the "firm-foundation" theory to ascertain if the stock represents real value. For example, suppose that Biodegradable Bottling Company is selling at ten times earnings, and the analyst estimates that it can sustain a long-term growth rate of 15 percent. If, on average, stocks with 15-percent anticipated growth rates are selling at seventeen times earnings, the fundamentalist might conclude that Biodegradable was a "cheap stock" and recommend purchase.

Does Charting Work?

We have seen in Chapter 1 that Lord Keynes made a fortune for Cambridge University by outguessing the investing actions of the crowd. Was this because he was a chartist or simply a brilliant forecaster of crowd reactions? The evidence suggests that his results were due to his brilliance. The truth is that no matter how impressive the technician's talk of bottoms, tops, and unmentionable parts in between, the talk has no basis in fact.

So much stock market history on prices and volume of trading is now readily available on computer tapes that it is possible to simulate and test various technical rules to see if there is momentum in the stock market. If stock prices have been going up, is it likely that they will go up in the future? Should you purchase relatively strong stocks and avoid those that have been acting poorly? Should you buy stocks that have just bounced up from their lows, and sell those that have fallen from their highs? Are any chart patterns reliable predictors of future price movements?

One set of tests, perhaps the simplest of all, compares the price change for a stock in a given period with the price change in a subsequent period. Technical lore has it that if the price of a stock rose yesterday, it is more likely to rise today. In other words, the sequence of price changes prior to any given day is important in predicting the price change for that day.

It turns out that the correlation of past price movements with present and future price movements is essentially zero. Yesterday's price change bears no relationship to the price change today. Last week's price change bears no relationship to the price change this week. Last month's price change bears no relationship to the price change this month, etc. Such tests have been made using stockprice data on both major exchanges going back as far as the beginning of the twentieth century. The results reveal conclusively that past movements in stock prices cannot be used to foretell future movements. The stock market has no memory. The central proposition of charting is absolutely false, and investors who follow its precepts will accomplish nothing but increasing substantially the brokerage charges they pay.

It is also possible to demonstrate the existence of leaks in another popular technical scheme based on the momentum principle—the so-called filter system. According to this system a stock that has reached a low point and has moved up, say, 5 percent (or any other percent you wish to name), is said to be in an uptrend. A stock that has reached a peak and has moved down 5 percent is said to be in a downtrend. You are supposed to buy any stock that has moved up 5 percent from its low and hold it until the price moves down 5 percent from a subsequent high, at which time you sell the stock. Through extensive computer simulation of various filter rules it was found that when the higher brokerage commissions incurred under the filter rules are taken into consideration, these techniques cannot consistently beat a policy of simply buying the individual stock (or the stock average in question) and holding it over the period during which the test is performed. The individual investor would do well to avoid employing any filter rule and, I might add, any broker who recommends it.

Many investors are convinced that the economists' disclaimer that chart patterns do not exist must be arrant nonsense. Anyone who reads the financial pages, with its charts of recent market activity, can readily attest that there are chart patterns and clear up and down trends in the stock market. For example, in *Random Walk,* I presented the stock chart shown in Figure 2.

The chart seems to display some obvious patterns of up and down trends. How can the economist be so myopic that he cannot see what is so plainly visible to the naked eye?

The persistence of this belief in repetitive patterns in the stock market is due to statistical illusion. To illustrate, let me describe an experiment in which I asked my students to participate. The students were asked to construct a normal stock chart showing the movements of a hypothetical stock initially selling at $50 per

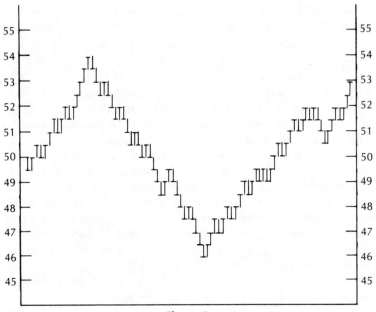

Figure 2.

share. For each successive trading day, the closing stock price would be determined by the flip of a fair coin. If the toss was a head, the students assumed that the stock closed ½ point higher than the preceding close. If the flip was a tail, the price was assumed to be down by ½. The chart displayed above was actually the hypothetical stock chart derived from one of these experiments.

The chart derived from random coin tossings looks remarkably like a normal stock price chart, and even appears to display cycles. Of course, the pronounced "cycles" that we seem to observe in coin tossings do not occur at regular intervals as true cycles do, but neither do the ups and downs in the stock market.

In other simulated stock charts derived from student coin tossings there were so-called head-and-shoulders formations, where the daily stock price movements seemed to form a shoulder, a head, and then another shoulder. In others, we found "triple tops," "double bottoms," and other more esoteric chart patterns. One of the charts showed a beautiful upward breakout from an inverted head and shoulders (a very bullish formation). I showed it to a chartist friend of mine who practically jumped out of his skin. "What is this company?" he exclaimed. "We've got to buy immediately." He did not respond kindly to me when I told him the chart had been produced by flipping a coin. (I got my comuppance when *Business Week* hired a technician, who was adept at hatchet work, to review my book.)

My students used a completely random process to produce their stock charts. With each toss, as long as the coins used were fair, there was a 50-percent chance of heads, implying an upward move in the price of the stock, and a 50-percent chance of tails and a downward move. Even if they flip ten heads in a row, the chance of getting a head on the next toss is still 50 percent. Mathematicians call a sequence of numbers produced by a random process (such as those on our simulated stock chart) a random walk. The next move on the chart is completely unpredictable on the basis of what has happened before.

Now, in fact, the stock market does not quite measure up to the mathematician's ideal of the complete independence of present price movements from those in the past. There have been some *very slight* dependencies found. But any systematic relationships that exist are so small that they are not useful for an investor. The brokerage charges involved in trying to take advantage of these dependencies are far greater than any advantage that might be obtained. This is the consistent finding of the academic research on stock prices. As my colleague Richard Quandt says, "Technical analysis is akin to astrology and every bit as scientific."

I am *not* saying that technical strategies never make money. They very often do make profits. The point is rather that a simple "buy-and-hold" strategy (that is, buying a stock or group of stocks and holding on for a long period of time) typically makes as much or more money.

Can more complicated technical systems then be profitably put to work? A number of more elaborate systems have also been tested. One of the earliest and best known technical systems is called the Dow Theory. It's somewhat similar to the filter system in that you buy when the market goes higher than its last peak and sell when it sinks through its preceding valley. Computer simulation has shown that the market's performance after *sell* signals is no different from its performance after *buy* signals. Once again, relative to simply buying and holding the representative list of stocks in the market averages, the Dow follower actually comes out a little behind, since the strategy entails a number of extra brokerage costs as the investor buys and sells when the strategy decrees.

Another popular technique is called the "relative-strength" system. Here an investor buys and holds those stocks that are acting well, that is, outperforming the general market indexes in the recent past. Conversely, the stocks that are acting poorly relative to the market should be avoided, or perhaps even sold short. While there do seem to be some time periods when a relative-strength strategy would have outperformed a buy-and-hold strategy, there is no evidence that it can do so consistently. A computer test of relative-strength rules over a twenty-five-year period suggests that such rules do not, after accounting for brokerage charges, outperform a buy-and-hold investment strategy.

Tests have also been made of a variety of price-volume systems, as well as schemes involving the recognition of specific chart patterns such as channels, wedges, heads and shoulders, triple bottoms, etc. Again, the investor following such systems is likely to be disappointed in the results. The buy and sell signals generated by the strategies contain no information useful to predicting future price movements. After accounting for brokerage charges, the investor does worse than he would by simply buying and holding a diversified group of stocks.

These and a multitude of other studies are remarkably similar in their findings. While not all studies are completely consistent with the theoretical ideal of randomness, they all suggest that no technical strategy can consistently outperform a buy-and-hold strategy after accounting for brokerage costs.

Why then is technical analysis—and charting—so popular? For one thing, it's colorful and makes for good copy in magazines and newspapers. Even more important, however, is that technicians often play an important role in the greening of the brokers. Chartists recommend trades—almost every technical system involves some degree of in-and-out trading. Trading generates commissions, and commissions are the lifeblood of the brokerage business. The technicians do not help produce yachts for the customers, but they do help generate the trading that provides yachts for the brokers. Until the public catches on to this bit of trickery, technicians will continue to flourish.

There have been many complaints about the thesis presented here. The most frequent go something like this: "The market isn't random and no mathematician is going to convince me it is. Dividends and earnings must influence stock prices."

Of course earnings and dividends influence market prices, and so does the temper of the crowd. The random walkers do not deny that a news event indicating unexpectedly higher earnings for a company will tend to raise the price of its stock. Indeed, the theory suggests that the market is an extremely efficient mechanism: so efficient, in fact, that it adjusts to such new information right away, not gradually over time forming a long uptrend. But new information about a company (a big mineral strike, the death of the president, etc.) is unpredictable. It will occur randomly over time. If an item of news were not random, that is, if it were *dependent* on an earlier item of news, then it wouldn't be news at all.

Technical analysts also argue that not all charting schemes have been tested. That is quite correct. No economist or statistician, however skillful, can prove conclusively that technical methods can never work. All that can be said is that the small amount of information contained in stock market pricing patterns has not been shown to be sufficient to overcome the brokerage costs involved in acting on that information.

Abandoning the precepts of my profession, I will state categorically, however, that no technical scheme whatever could work for any length of time. I suggest first that methods which people are convinced "really work" have not been adequately tested; and second, that even if they did work the schemes would be bound to destroy themselves.

If you examine past stock prices in any given period, you can almost always find some kind of system that would have worked in a given period. During the decade of the 1970s, for example, it is quite possible that stocks starting with the letters B or S and with daily volume over 10,000 shares have outperformed the averages. Obviously, it is always possible to describe, after the fact, which categories of stocks had the best performance. The real problem is, of course, whether the scheme works in a different time period. What most advocates of technical analysis usually fail to do is to test their schemes with market data derived from other periods than those during which the scheme was developed.

Even if the technician follows my advice by testing his scheme in many different time periods and finds it a reliable predictor of stock prices, I still believe that technical analysis must ultimately be worthless. For the sake of argument, suppose the technician had found that there was a reliable year-end rally, that is, every year stock prices rose between Christmas and New Year's Day. The problem is that once such a regularity is known to market participants, people will act in a way that prevents it from happening in the future.

Any successful technical scheme must ultimately self-destruct. The moment I realize that prices will be higher after New Year's Day than they are before Christmas, I will start buying before Christmas ever comes around. If people know a stock will go up *tomorrow*, you can be sure it will go up *today*. Any regularity in the stock market that can be discovered and acted upon profitably is bound to destroy itself. This is the fundamental reason why I am convinced that no one will be successful in employing technical methods to make money in the stock market.

The implications of this analysis are simple. If past prices contain no useful information for the prediction of future prices, there is no point in following any technical trading rule for timing the purchases and sales of securities. Discontinue your subscriptions to worthless technical services, and eschew brokers who read charts and are continually recommending the purchase or sale of securities. Simply buying and holding a diversified portfolio suited to your objectives will enable you to save on investment expense, brokerage charges, and also taxes, since short-term capital gains are taxed at regular income tax rates. At the same time, you will achieve an overall performance record at least as good as that obtainable using technical methods.

Does Fundamental Security Analysis Work?

In a sense, the preceding studies are not too surprising. Most respectable people on Wall Street have long believed that technicians were a rather weird group anyway, and put little stock in their recommendations. Besides, most technicians have holes in their shoes. The question that really gets the Wall Streeter where he lives is whether fundamental analysis is any good. So let us now take on the fundamental analysts.

Remember, the first job of the security analyst is to predict future growth for companies he follows. A first step is usually to look at the past record. Some really simpleminded fundamentalists predict the future by extrapolating the past.

That's not a very good idea. As it turns out, the growth rates for companies from one period to the next are essentially uncorrelated. If you know the growth rates of all companies over, say, the 1960–70 period, this would have been no help at all to you in predicting what growth they achieved in the 1970–80 period. This result was first established by Ian Little for British companies in his charmingly titled article "Higgledy-Piggledy Growth." It was later confirmed for U.S. companies in a study at Princeton. No matter how long the period involved, past growth is useless in predicting future growth. The IBMs of this world are the rare exceptions, not the rule. And for every IBM I'll give you a Polaroid—a growth company that stumbled badly in the 1970s. Indeed, even IBM itself had a slight slip in 1979.

More thorough-minded analysts do not just project past growth. They do a thorough study and analysis of all relevant industry and company factors before estimating future growth rates. Surely these careful estimates of the security analysts must be better than the past growth-rate extrapolations if the analysts are worth their salt.

At Princeton's Financial Research Center, we donned the cloak of academic neutrality and collected the growth-rate estimates (both one-year and five-year) made by security analysts from nineteen different investment firms—major banks, investment bankers, brokers, and mutual fund management companies. While the analysts did do somewhat better than simple extrapolations of past growth, their overall record was poor. When compared with actual long-term earnings growth rates that were subsequently realized, the estimates of the security analysts were worse than several naïve forecasting models. For example, you would sometimes do better simply predicting that each company would grow at the rate of the overall national income of the country rather than take the analysts' estimates. Even more surprising, the analysts' one-year forecasts were even worse than their five-year projections.

The analysts gamely fought back. They complained that it was unfair to judge their performance on a wide cross section of industries, since earnings for electronics firms and various "cyclical" companies are notoriously hard to forecast. "Try us on utilities," one analyst confidently asserted. So we tried it, and they didn't like it. Even the forecasts for the stable utilities were far off the mark. Those the analysts confidently touted as high growers turned out to perform much the same as the utilities for which only low or moderate growth was predicted. This led to the second major finding of our study: there is not one industry that is easy to predict.

The third finding was that analysts who did better than average one year were no more likely than the others to make superior forecasts in the next year. The implication for investors is this: security analysts have enormous difficulty in forecasting earnings prospects for the companies they follow. Investors who put blind faith in such forecasts in making their investment selections are in for some rude disappointments.

The real test of fundamental analysts, however, lies in the performance of the stocks they recommend for their clients. Fortunately, records are available for one group of professionals— the mutual funds who employ large staffs of the best paid fundamental security analysts in selecting their portfolios. Analysis of the data shows that investors have done no better with the average mutual fund than they could have done by purchasing and holding an unmanaged broad stock index. In other words, over long periods of time mutual fund portfolios have not outperformed randomly selected groups of stocks.

In addition to the scientific evidence that has been accumulated, several less formal tests have verified this finding. The editors of *Forbes* magazine, for example, intrigued with the results of academic studies, have now for several years followed the results of a portfolio of common stocks chosen by throwing darts. The magazine announced the 1979 results with a bit of glee: "Well, we did it again. Forbes' 'Dart Board Fund' has once more beaten the averages and most of the professional money managers." Does this mean that the wrist is mightier than the brain? Perhaps not, but I think that the *Forbes*'s editors raise a very valid question when they conclude, "it would seem that a combination of luck and sloth beats brains."

How can this be? Every year one can read the performance rankings of mutual funds. These *always* show a substantial number of funds beating the averages each year—and some by significant amounts. The problem is that there is no consistency to the performance. A manager who has been better than average one year has only a 50-percent chance of doing better than average in the next year. Just as past earnings growth cannot predict future earnings, neither can past fund performance predict future results. Fund managements are also subject to random events—they may grow fat, become lazy, or break up. An investment approach that works very well for one period can easily turn sour the next. One is tempted to conclude that a very important factor in determining poll ranking is our old friend Lady Luck.

To shed further light on this issue, Table 5 updates some results first presented in my *Random Walk* book. It shows the top twenty funds in 1968 and then follows their record over the next six years.

I mentioned in Chapter 1 that performance investing was a product of the 1960s and became especially prominent during the 1967–68 strong bull market. Capital preservation had given way to capital productivity. The fund managers who turned in the best results for the period were written up in the financial press like sports celebrities. When the performance polls were published in 1967 and 1968, the go-go funds with their youthful gunslingers as managers and concept stocks as investments were right at the top of the pack, outgunning all the competition by a wide margin.

The game ended unceremoniously with the bear market that commenced in 1969 and continued until 1971. The go-go funds suddenly went into reverse. It was fly now and pay later for the performance funds. Their portfolios of volatile concept stocks were no exception to the financial law of gravity. They went down just as sharply as they had gone up. The legendary brilliance of the fund managers turned out to be mainly a legend of their own creation. The top funds in 1968 had a perfectly disastrous performance in the ensuing years (I was not able to extend my table after 1974 because by 1975 many of the funds were no longer in business).

The Mates Fund, for example, was number one in 1968. At the end of 1974, the Mates Fund sold at about one-fifteenth of its 1968 value and Mates finally threw in the towel. He then left the investment community to enter a business catering to a new fad. In New York City he started a singles' bar, appropriately named "Mates."

It seems clear that one cannot count on consistency of performance. Unlike the Montréal Canadiens, portfolio managers do not *consistently* outdistance their rivals. (In fact, sometimes even the Habs lose.) But I must be fair: there are exceptions to the rule. Note portfolio manager number nineteen on Table 5.

TABLE 5
Some Results of the Performance Derby

1968 Rank	Fund	1969 rank[e]	1970 rank[e]	1971 rank[e]	1972 rank[e]	1973 rank[e]	1974 rank[e]	1968 Net asset value[f] per share	1974 Net asset value per share
1	Mates Investment Fund	312	424	512	465	531	400	15.51	1.12
2	Neuwirth Fund	263	360	104	477	397	232	15.29	6.24
3	Gibraltar Growth Fund[a]	172	456	481				17.27	
4	Insurance Investors Fund[b]	77	106	317	417	224		7.45	
5	Pennsylvania Mutual	333	459	480	486	519	521	11.92	1.09
6	Puerto Rican Investors Fund[a]	30	308	387	435			19.34	
7	Crown Western-Dallas	283	438	207	244	330	133	13.86	4.66
8	Franklin Dynatech Series	342	363	112	120	453	453	14.47	4.56
9	First Participating Fund[c]	49	283	106	27	220	310	19.25	13.47

10	Connecticut Western Mutual Fund[d]	5	202	133	364	250	416	127.27	3.84
11	Enterprise Fund	334	397	233	161	312	443	11.88	4.58
12	Ivy Fund	357	293	62	62	127	428	12.37	8.48
13	Century Shares Trust	120	55	152	452	62	4	13.09	15.44
14	Mutual Shares Corp.	284	272	45	54	354	211	22.18	6.42
15	Putnam Equities Fund	376	384	277	231	35	90	17.05	4.73
16	Financial Industrial Income Fund	244	222					8.40	
17	Consumers Investment[a]	354						6.21	
18	Columbia Growth Fund	33	322	27	370	332	253	14.23	9.05
19	Templeton Growth Fund	1	241	163	1	81	84	4.00	6.23
20	Schuster Fund	129	231	253	425	445	434	12.29	4.86

SOURCE: Lipper Analytical Division, Lipper Analytical Services, Inc.

[a]No longer surveyed by Lipper.

[b]Insurance Investors Fund later changed name to First Sierra Fund. No longer surveyed by Lipper.

[c]First Participating Fund is now American General Growth Fund.

[d]Connecticut Western is now Channing Bond Fund, which is no longer surveyed by Lipper.

[e]Out of 381 funds surveyed in 1969, 463 in 1970, 526 in 1971, 537 in 1972, 536 in 1973, and 527 in 1974.

[f]The net asset values for 1968 have been adjusted for all subsequent splits.

The Templeton Growth Fund has been a superior performer not only during the period covered in the table but also in other periods as well. It is an excellent counterexample to the rule—but it is very rare. I will discuss this particular fund (as well as some other rare exceptions) in Chapter 5.

While the above results have all focused on mutual funds, it should not be assumed that the funds are simply the worst of the whole lot of investment managers. In fact, the mutual funds have had a somewhat *better* performance record than many other professional investors. The records of life insurance companies, property and casualty insurance companies, foundations, college endowments, state and local trust funds, personal trusts administered by banks, and individual discretionary accounts handled by investment advisors have all been studied, although not in nearly the same detail as mutual funds. This research suggests that there are no sizable differences in the investment performance of any of these professional investors or between the investment performance of these groups and that of the market as a whole. As in the case of the mutual funds there are some exceptions, but again they are very rare. *No scientific evidence has yet been assembled to indicate that the investment performance of professionally managed portfolios as a group has been any better than that of randomly selected portfolios.*

Why Shouldn't the Professional Managers Have a Big Edge?

We have seen that professional investment managers relying as they do on "fundamental analysis" are no more effective than technical analysts in beating the market. Paradoxically, the reason for the failure of professional investment management may not be the incompetence of the investment professional but rather his acumen and swiftness. Fundamental analysis may be no more effective than technical analysis not because it is worthless, but rather because it is self-defeating. Information is disseminated so rapidly today that market prices react almost im-

mediately. The time between the word (news) and the deed (buying a stock) has become so infinitesimal that it is almost impossible to realize a significant profit in the stock market on the basis
of fundamental analysis. The market is simply too efficient.

Nobel laureate Paul Samuelson sums up the situation as follows:

> If intelligent people are constantly shopping around for good value,
> selling those stocks they think will turn out to be overvalued and buying
> those they expect are now undervalued, the result of this action by
> intelligent investors will be to have existng stock prices already have
> discounted in them an allowance for their future prospects. Hence, to
> the passive investor, who does not himself search out for under- and
> overvalued situations, there will be presented a pattern of stock prices
> that makes one stock about as good or bad a buy as another. To that
> passive investor, chance alone would be as good a method of selection
> as anything else.

This is the efficient-market theory. It says that all that is known
concerning the expected growth of the company's earnings and
dividends, all of the possible favorable and unfavorable developments affecting the company that might be studied by the fundamental analyst, are already reflected in the price of the company's
stock. Thus throwing darts at the financial page will produce a
portfolio that can be expected to do as well as any managed by
professional security analysts.

Now I must admit to being not quite as ready as my academic
colleagues to damn the entire field. While it is abundantly clear
that the pros do not consistently beat the averages, I still worry
about accepting all the tenets of the efficient-market theory, in
part because the theory rests on several fragile assumptions. The
first is that perfect pricing exists. As the quote from Paul Samuelson indicates, the theory holds that at any time stocks sell at the
best estimates of their intrinsic values. Thus, uninformed investors buying at today's structure of prices are really getting full
value for their money, whatever securities they purchase.

This line of reasoning is uncomfortably close to that of the "greater fool" theory. We have seen ample evidence in Chapter 1 that stocks sometimes do not sell on the basis of anyone's estimate of value (as hard as this is to measure) but are often swept up in waves of frenzy. Even the market pros were largely responsible for several speculative waves of the 1960s and 1970s. The existence of these broader influences on market prices at least raises the possibility that investors might not want to accept the current tableau of market prices as being the best reflection of intrinsic values.

Another fragile assumption is that news travels instantaneously. I doubt that there will ever be a time in the future when all useful inside information is immediately disclosed to all. Indeed, even if it can be argued that all relevant news for the major stocks followed by institutional investors gets quickly impounded into their prices, it may well be that this is not the case for all the thousands of small companies that are not closely followed by the pros. Moreover, the efficient-market theory implies that no one possesses monopolistic power over the market and that stock recommendations based on unfounded beliefs do not lead to large buying. But brokerage firms specializing in research services to institutions wield considerable power in the market and can direct tremendous money flows in and out of stocks. In this environment it is quite possible that erroneous beliefs about a stock by some professionals can for a considerable time be self-fulfilling.

Finally, there is the enormous difficulty of translating known information about a stock into estimates of true value. We have seen that the major determinants of a stock's value concern the extent and duration of its growth path far into the future. This is an extraordinarily difficult estimate to make and there is considerable scope for an individual to exercise superior intellect and judgment to turn in superior performance.

But while I believe in the possibility of superior professional investment performance, I must emphasize that the evidence we have thus far does not support the view that such competence exists; and while I may be excommunicated from some academic sects because of my only lukewarm endorsement of the efficient-market theory, I make no effort to disguise my heresy in the financial church. It is clear that if there are exceptional financial managers, they are very rare. This is a fact of life with which both individual and institutional investors will have to deal.

Risk Has Its Reward

While there is no dependable relationship between superior performance from one period to the next, there is one systematic relationship concerning investment performance. One of the best documented propositions in the field of finance is that, on average, investors receive higher rates of return for bearing greater risk. Indeed, what differences there are in the long-run returns realized by different professional managers can almost entirely be explained by differences in the risk they have taken.

Unfortunately, the term "risk" is a most slippery and elusive concept. It is hard for economists, let alone investors, to agree on a precise definition. Risk is usually associated with the possibility of suffering harm or loss. An investor who buys one-year Treasury bills to yield 9 percent and holds them until they mature is virtually certain of earning a 9-percent return over that one-year time period. The possibility of loss is so small as to be considered nonexistent.[1] However, if the investor holds common stock in a local power and light company for one year on the basis of an anticipated 11-percent dividend return, the possibility of loss increases. The dividend of the company might be cut and, more important, the market price of the stock at the end of the year could be much lower, resulting in serious net loss for the investor. Risk is the chance that expected returns from securities or other assets will not materialize and, in particular, that one's investments may fall in value.

Once academics accepted the idea that risk for investors is

[1]Of course, the investor can lose in real purchasing power if the inflation rate exceeds 9 percent, but there is no risk of losing the specific number of dollars invested.

related to the chance of disappointment in achieving expected security returns, a natural measure suggested itself—the probable variability or dispersion of future returns. Thus, financial risk has generally been defined as the variance or standard deviation of returns.[2] Very careful studies have been made relating past returns on stocks and bonds to the dispersion of those returns. The results confirm our expectations.

One of the most thorough recent studies was done by Roger Ibbotson and Rex Sinquefield. Their data covered the period 1926 through 1978. The results are shown in Table 6. The table is not designed to show a series of Eiffel Towers and one Manhattan skyline. What Ibbotson and Sinquefield did was to take several different investment forms—stocks, bonds, and Treasury bills—as well as the consumer price index, and measure the percentage increase or decrease each year for each item. A rectangle was then erected on the baseline to indicate the number of years the returns fell between 0 and 5 percent, another rectangle indicating the number of years the returns fell between 5 and 10 percent, and so on, for both positive and negative returns. The result is a chart which shows the dispersion of returns and from which the standard deviation can be calculated.

A quick glance shows that, over long periods of time, common stocks have, on average, provided relatively generous total rates of return. These returns, including dividends and capital gains, have exceeded by a substantial margin the returns from long-term corporate bonds. The stock returns have also tended to be well in excess of the inflation rate as measured by the annual rate of increase in consumer prices. Thus, stocks have also tended to provide positive "real" rates of return, that is, returns after washing out the effects of inflation. The data show, however, that common stock returns are highly variable as measured by the "standard deviation" and the range of annual returns shown in

---

[2]Those who may have suffered through a statistics course at some time in life may recall that the variance is defined as the average squared difference of each of the return numbers from its mean. The standard deviation is the square root of the variance.

TABLE 6

Selected Performance Statistics: 1926–78

Series	Annual (geometric) mean rate of return	Number of years returns are positive	Number of years returns are negative	Highest annual return (and year)	Lowest annual return (and year)	Standard deviation of annual returns	Distribution
Common stocks	8.9	35	18	54.0% (1933)	−43.3 (1931)	22.4	
Long-term corporate bonds	4.0	43	10	18.4 (1970)	−8.1 (1969)	5.8	
U.S. Treasury bills	2.5	52	1	8.0 (1974)	−0.0 (1940)	2.1	
Consumer Price Index	2.5	43	10	18.2 (1946)	−10.3 (1932)	4.7	

SOURCE: Roger G. Ibbotson and Rex A. Sinquefield, *Stocks, Bonds, Bills, and Inflation.*

the last two columns of Table 6. Returns from equities have ranged from a gain of over 50 percent (in 1933) to a loss of almost the same magnitude (in 1931). Clearly, the extra returns that have been available to investors from stocks have come at the expense of assuming considerably higher risk.

There have also been several periods of five years or longer when common stocks have actually produced negative rates of return. Indeed, almost the entire past decade has been an extremely poor one for the stock market. The 40-percent decline in the broad stock market averages from January 1973 through February 1974 is the most dramatic change in stock prices during a brief period since the 1930s. From late 1976 through early 1978 the market had another serious sinking spell with the popular averages down more than 20 percent. Still, over the long pull, investors have been rewarded with higher returns for taking on more risk.

The patterns evident in Ibbotson's and Sinquefield's chart also appear when the returns and risks of individual stock portfolios are compared. Indeed, the differences that exist in the returns from different funds can be explained almost entirely by differences in the risk they have taken. Figure 3 illustrates this relationship over the 1965–78 period for representative groups of institutionally managed funds. Figure 4 illustrates the relationship for a large group of common stock mutual funds during the five-year period from the end of 1974 to the end of 1979.

In the figures, risk is measured in a slightly different manner from Table 6. Instead of total variability (standard deviation) we measure risk in terms of relative volatility, that is, variability relative to the stock market as a whole. This risk measure is more popularly known in the language of the new investment technology as *beta*. The beta calculation is essentially a comparison between the movements of a portfolio (or individual stock) and the movements of the market as a whole.

To make a beta calculation, you take a broad market index such as the S&P 500 and assign it a value of one. A stock or portfolio with a beta of 1 will tend to swing as the market does, a sort of

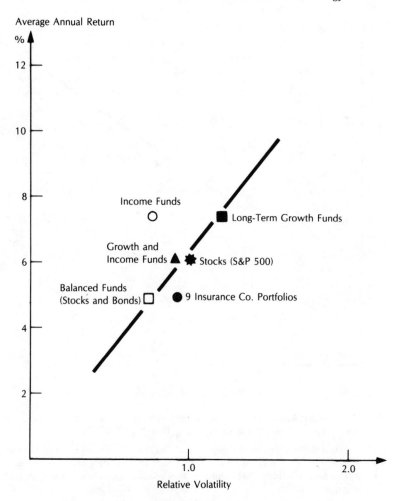

Figure 3. *Average Annual Return vs. Risk: Selected Institutional Investors (14 Years, 1965–1978).*

SOURCE: Buck Consultants, Inc.

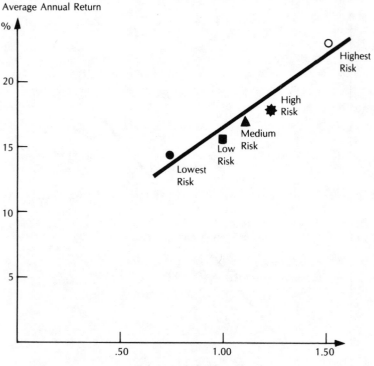

Figure 4. *Average Annual Return vs. Common Stock Mutual Funds Grouped by Risk Level.*

SOURCE: Computer Direction's Advisers, Inc. Betas are for three years to November 30, 1979; performance represents total return for five years to November 30, 1979. The survey includes 261 common stock mutual funds. Funds are grouped by beta quintiles.

"Me and My Shadow" combination. A beta of two, however, means that your investment is twice as volatile as the market: if the market goes up 5 percent, it tends to go up 10 percent; if the market goes down 10 percent, it tends to lose a whopping 20 percent. A beta of 0.5 is for those who like to go to bed very early in the evening: when the market goes down 10 percent, the 0.5 beta investment generally sinks only by 5 percent. But as we know, where there is less risk there is less reward, and this same portfolio will only climb by 5 percent when the market goes up by 10 percent. Professionals often call high-beta portfolios "aggressive and risky" portfolios, and label low-beta portfolios as "defensive and relatively safer."

In the revised edition of *A Random Walk Down Wall Street,* I explain the rationale for using beta as a measure of risk. The guts of the argument is that beta is a measure of the irreducible variability in investment returns that results from market swings and that can not be eliminated through diversification of your holdings. Since this risk cannot be diversified away, the new investment technology believes that investors will be rewarded for bearing this risk with some additional return.

Figures 3 and 4 show the relationship between performance and the beta measure of relative volatility. Over the long pull, high-beta portfolios have provided larger total returns than low-risk ones. Similar kinds of results have been found for other time periods and for a variety of actual and simulated portfolios. The beta of a portfolio does seem to be not only a useful risk measure but also a good predictor of the long-run rate of return to be expected from that portfolio.

The possibility of obtaining higher returns over the long pull from higher beta portfolios is perfectly consistent with the efficient-market notions I discussed earlier. The efficient-market theory asserts that there is no way to gain superior performance (that is, extra returns) for a given *level of risk.* Believers in the new investment technology say that the only way to gain extra returns is to take on more risk. But this is hardly an inefficiency in the market. It is the natural expectation in a market where most participants dislike risk and therefore must be compensated (re-warded) to bear it.

The New Investment Technology

The combined notions of markets being efficient and invest-ment rewards being related to risk (beta) are what is now known as the new investment technology (NIT).

Just as particular types of stocks have had their fads, so did NIT. The *Institutional Investor,* the glossy prestige magazine that spent most of its pages chronicling the accomplishments of pro-fessional money managers, put its imprimatur on the movement in 1971 by featuring on its cover the letters BETA on top of a temple and including as its lead story "The Beta Cult! The New Way to Measure Risk." The magazine noted that money men whose mathematics hardly went beyond long division were now "tossing betas around with the abandon of Ph.D.s in statistical theory." Even the Securities and Exchange Commission gave beta its approval as a risk measure in its *Institutional Investor Study.*

In Wall Street the early beta fans boasted that they could earn higher long-run rates of return simply by buying a few high-beta stocks. Those who thought they were able to time the market thought they had an even better idea. They would buy high-beta stocks when they thought the market was going up, switching to low-beta ones when they feared the market might decline. To accommodate the enthusiasm for this new investment idea, beta measurement services proliferated among brokers, and it was a symbol of progressiveness for an investment house to provide its own beta estimates.[3] The beta boosters in "the street" oversold their product with an abandon that would have shocked even the

[3]Beta numbers are available from many brokers, including Merrill Lynch, Pierce, Fenner and Smith and the Value Line Investment Survey. The beta esti-mates are actually obtained by finding the relationship between the volatility of a particular stock and the market over a number of years in the past.

most enthusiastic academic scribblers intent on spreading the beta gospel.

How Good Is Beta as a Measure of Risk?

Is beta all it's cracked up to be as a useful measure of risk and predictor of future returns? Or is it simply a tool akin to technical analysis—a bastard cousin of the chartists? Is it always true that high-beta portfolios will, over the long pull, provide larger overall returns than lower beta risk ones, as the new investment technology suggests? And does a beta value calculated on the basis of past history really give you any useful information about future betas? These are subjects of intense current debate among practitioners and academics, and all the evidence is not yet in. Nevertheless, the tentative conclusion, based on what we now know, is encouraging.

It turns out that beta estimates for individual stocks are not very accurate, and that is one reason many professionals say nasty things about beta. The people who oversold beta as a useful tool in predicting the behavior of individual stocks did the beta cause a great disservice.

Thanks to the law of large numbers, however, a number of inaccurate beta estimates on individual stocks can be combined to form surprisingly accurate estimates of the risk of a portfolio. While the beta estimates for some securities will be much too high, the estimates for many others will be too low. The result is that the average beta in a well-defined portfolio is a good predictor of performance. And as we have seen earlier, *long-run* returns are higher for portfolios with higher beta values.

Yes, beta does seem to be a useful risk measure, but it's far from perfect. While there is little doubt that security and portfolio returns are related to risk as measured by beta, not all the empirical evidence is as uniformly favorable as the studies I have reported so far. For one thing, beta does not always perform well in the short run. There have been periods when safer (lower beta) stocks went up more than more volatile securities. It seems clear that while beta does do a good job in predicting a long-run relationship, it cannot be used to guarantee investors a predictable performance over periods of a few months or even a year.

Finally, there have been serious questions raised regarding how to measure beta, what market index to use in calculating relative volatility, and even whether beta is the appropriate measure of risk. To the great relief of assistant professors who must publish or perish, there is still much debate within the academic community on risk measurement, and much more empirical testing needs to be done. It is clear, however, that beta is not perfect and caution is required to ensure that the tool is not oversold as the final answer to the problems of building portfolios and projecting their risks and rewards. In judging risk, beta cannot be a substitute for brains.

As one might expect, there has been a tremendous amount of recent work by NIT followers to try to improve our risk-measurement techniques. One of the most celebrated of these workers is Barr Rosenberg, a professor at Berkeley, whose NIT work and laid-back California lifestyle were celebrated in another cover story of *Institutional Investor* during the late 1970s. What Rosenberg has done is to come up with a new risk-measurement system including a better beta mousetrap. Instead of calculating betas from past history, Rosenberg calculates what he calls "fundamental betas" based on the fundamental characteristics of each company, such as its earnings history relative to size, financial structure, and so forth. (Think of Chrysler, a relatively small company in a cyclical industry, in debt up to its eyeballs. No wonder the stock is so volatile.) Widely respected in the trade, these risk estimates are known as "Barr's bionic betas."

An academic turned entrepreneur, Rosenberg has formed his own firm, Barr Rosenberg and Associates (or just BARRA, as it appears on the official company T-shirt). Along with his reputation as the guru of NIT, Barr presents the perfect image. He is into Zen, he attends Essalen, and intones a Sanskrit chant before dinner. He believes in telepathy and clairvoyance. Each year, he spends three months on the Hawaiian island of Kauai for work and meditation. Although quiet and unassuming, he projects a kind of authority and omniscience. While the pros have not all jumped to embrace Rosenberg's techniques, he has won several converts among the cadre of institutional investors.

So we see that risk and return are related, and important improvements have been made in the techniques of risk measurement. Still, we must be careful not to accept beta or any other simple measure as an easy way to assess risk and to predict future returns with any certainty. You should know about the best of the modern techniques of NIT—they can be useful aids. But there is never going to be a handsome genie that will appear to solve all your investment problems. And even if he did, we would probably foul it up—as did the little old lady in the following favorite story of Robert Kirby of Capital Guardian Trust:

She was sitting in her rocking chair on the porch of the retirement home when a little genie appeared and said, "I've decided to grant you three wishes."

The little old lady answered, "Buzz off, you little twerp, I've seen all the wise guys I need to in my life."

The genie answered, "Look, I'm not kidding. This is for real. Just try me."

She shrugged and said, "Okay, turn my rocking chair into solid gold."

When, in a puff of smoke, he did it, her interest picked up noticeably. She said, "Turn me into a beautiful young maiden."

Again, in a puff of smoke, he did it. Finally, she said, "Okay, for my third wish turn my cat into a handsome young price."

In an instant, there stood the young prince, who then turned to her and asked, "Now aren't you sorry you had me fixed?"

CHAPTER 3

Ten Investment
Commandments to Keep
Ahead of Inflation

Securities markets are both logical and psychological. Prices
can at times soar well above and fall far below their firm foundations of value. Yet looked at over long periods, markets appear
to be reasonably efficient. Over the long run there does seem to
be a relationship between investment rewards and risks. We need
both these lessons in devising a strategy to combat inflation. It's
time now to describe that strategy.

In this chapter, I offer ten investment commandments. You'll
need the highest possible returns on your investment funds to
keep up with inflation. If inflation continues at a 10-percent rate,
the price level will double and your dollars will lose half their
value in just seven years. By faithfully practicing my investment
commandments you will reduce your income taxes and risk, and
at the same time increase your returns and security. But before
we can begin on these inflation-beating strategies, we first must
prepare ourselves. Hence, the first commandments are just as
important as the last.

I. Cover Thyself with Protection

Disraeli once wrote that "patience is a necessary ingredient of genius." It's also a key element in investing; you can't afford to pull your money out at the wrong time. You need staying power to increase your odds of earning attractive long-run returns. That's why it is so important for you to have noninvestment resources, such as medical and life insurance, to draw on should any emergency strike you or your family. It isn't always the guy in the well-known TV commercial who is hit by misfortune and calls "Hello, Prudential." It could happen to you.

Did I just say insurance was a *noninvestment* resource? That's right: buy insurance policies for protection, not for the accumulation of assets. Some life insurance policies are like the common hot dog: once you know all the ingredients, you might prefer to do without them. I favor low-cost "term insurance" over higher premium whole-life policies. Check your insurance policy carefully. The term "living benefits" could be the tipoff that you should be investing in the life insurance firm's stocks and not paying its premiums. With "living benefits" you are buying an insurance scheme that is combined with a type of savings plan. The benefit goes to the seller, not to the buyer, because these plans pay interest rates on the savings portion that are far below the levels that could be earned if your money were invested directly in other assets. For example, if you buy a low-premium term insurance policy and invest the difference in annual premiums in safe bonds yourself, you should come out far ahead.

Buy renewable term insurance; you can keep renewing your policy without the need for a physical examination. This provides death benefits alone and no buildup of cash value. So-called decreasing term insurance, renewable for progressively lower amounts, should suit many families best since, as time passes (and the children and family resources grow), the need for protection usually diminishes. Unless you will incur heavy penalties for discontinuing your present coverage, or unless you are able to save money only if you get a bill from your insurance company, look for a term insurance plan. Use the money you save for the investments I'll discuss below.

You'll be surprised how much money you can often save by buying life insurance directly, rather than having an agent sell it to you. For example, some states have low-cost savings bank life insurance, which you can buy at your local savings institution. Agents, like stockbrokers, make their money on sales commissions. In a sense, they earn it by doing work that you could be doing yourself.

You should also keep some reserves in safe and liquid investments. That surely, to many, is the antithesis of investing. Why put money in a safe place when you could be picking the next winner on the stock market. To cover unforeseen emergencies, that's why! It's the height of folly to gamble that nothing will happen to you. Every family unit should have a reserve of funds to finance an unexpected medical bill or to provide a cushion during a time of unemployment.

The old rule of thumb was that a year's living expenses should be kept in assets that could be converted to cash quickly and without loss. If you are protected by medical and disability insurance, this emergency reserve can be reduced safely. Indeed, even some bank trust departments—the acme of conservative money management—now estimate that three months of living expenses are satisfactory. In no case, however, should you be without at least some assets near the safe and liquid end of the spectrum.

I know it may sound "old hat" to suggest that you hold liquid assets during a time of inflation when money depreciates. But I'll show you later how to earn yields of better than 10 percent on these funds during inflationary market conditions. And borrowing alternatives open to individuals needing immediate funds, such as borrowing on your credit cards, can cost you 18 percent per year or more. You are not likely to keep ahead of inflation by borrowing at those rates.

II. Know Thyself

This is a step in the investment process too many people skip over with disastrous results. You must decide at the outset what degree of risk you are willing to assume and what kinds of investments are most suitable to your tax brackets. The securities markets are like a large restaurant with a variety of products suitable for different tastes and needs. Just as there is no one food that is best for everyone, there is no one investment that is best for all investors.

We would all like to double our capital overnight, but how many of us can afford to see half our capital disintegrate just as quickly? J. P. Morgan once had a friend who was so worried about his stock holdings that he could not sleep at night. The friend asked, "What should I do about my stocks?" Morgan replied, "Sell down to the sleeping point." He wasn't kidding. Every investor must decide the trade-off he or she is willing to make between eating well and sleeping well. The decision is up to you. High investment rewards can be achieved only at the cost of substantial risk taking. This was the fundamental lesson of Chapter 2. So what's your sleeping point? Knowing thyself, and thus the answer to this question, is the first and one of the most important investment steps you must take.

To help raise your investment consciousness, I've prepared Table 7, on investment risk and expected return as of the start of the 1980s. At the stultifying end of the spectrum are a variety of short-term investments. Savings accounts appear to be the safest investment of all. You are *certain* to be able to withdraw every dollar you put in. The dollar value of your investment will never fluctuate. But even these investments do have a risk because in today's high-inflation era you are unfortunately just about certain to lose out in real purchasing power even with the interest added. Next come special six-month certificates and money-market funds—somewhat riskier investments, but far more likely to offer inflation protection. If this is your sleeping point and you wish to read no further, you'll find more information on these investments in Commandment V.

Corporate bonds present a riskier form of investment and some dreams will start intruding in your sleep pattern at this point. Good-quality, long-term public utility bonds now yield about 11½ percent when held to maturity. Should you sell before then, your return will depend on the level of interest rates at the

TABLE 7

The Sleeping Scale of Major Investment Choices

Sleeping point	Type of asset	Expected rate of return (1980) (before income taxes)	Length of time investment must be held to get expected rate of return	Risk level
Semicomatose state	Savings accounts	5½%	No specific investment period required. Many thrift institutions calculate interest from day of deposit to day of withdrawal.	No risk at losing what you put in. Deposits up to $40,000 guaranteed by an agency of the federal government. An almost sure loser with today's inflation, however.
Long afternoon naps and sound night's sleep	Special six-month certificates	11–12%	Money must be left on deposit for the entire six-months to take advantage of higher rate	Early withdrawals subject to penalty. Rates geared to expected inflation.
Sound night's sleep	Money-market funds	11–13%	No specific investment period required. Most funds provide check-writing privileges.	Very little since most funds are invested in bank certificates. Not guaranteed, however. Rates geared to expected inflation.

| Some occasional dream or two during an otherwise restful night | Corporate bonds (good-quality public utilities) | 11½% | Investments must be made for the period until the maturity of the bond (20–30 years) to be assured of the stated rate. The bonds may be sold at any time, however, in which case the net return will depend on fluctuations in the market price of the bonds. | Very little if held to maturity. Moderate fluctuations can be expected in realized return if bonds are sold prior to maturity. Rate geared to expected long-run inflation rate now. This may differ from *actual* rate over the term to maturity of the bond. |
| Some tossing and turning before you doze and vivid dreams upon awakening | Diversified portfolios of blue-chip common stocks (such as an index fund) | 15% | No specific investment periods required, and stocks may be sold at any time. The 15% average expected return assumes a fairly long investment period and can only be treated as a rough guide based on current conditions. | Moderate to substantial. In any one year the actual return could in fact be negative. Diversified portfolios have at times lost 25% or more of their actual value. Contrary to current opinion—a good inflation hedge. |

TABLE 7

The Sleeping Scale of Major Investment Choices (continued)

Sleeping point	Type of asset	Expected rate of return (1980) (before income taxes)	Length of time investment must be held to get expected rate of return	Risk level
Nightmares not uncommon, but over the long run well rested	Diversified portfolios of relatively risky stocks (such as aggressive growth-oriented mutual funds)	16–18%	Same as above. The average expected return of 16–18% assumes a fairly long investment period and can only be treated as a rough guide based on current conditions.	Substantial. In any one year the actual return could be negative. Diversified portfolios of very risky stocks have at times lost 50% or more of their value. Good inflation hedge.
Vivid dreams and occasional nightmares	Real estate	Similar to common stocks	Only makes sense as a very long-term investment. Heavy transactions costs in trading.	Can't sell in a hurry without substantial penalties. Hard to diversify. Very good inflation hedge if bought at reasonable price levels.
Bouts of insomnia	Gold	Impossible to predict	As long as there are greater fools to be found.	Enormous at today's price levels. Believed to be a hedge against doomsday.

time of sale. If they are higher than 11½ percent, your bonds will fall to a price that makes their yield competitive with new bonds offering a higher stated interest rate. Thus, there is a chance of loss. Your capital loss could be enough to eat up a whole year's interest—or even more. On the other hand, if interest rates fall, the price of your bonds will rise and you will not only get the promised 11½ percent interest but also a capital gain. Thus, if you sell prior to maturity, your actual yearly return could vary considerably, and that is why bonds are riskier than short-term instruments, which carry almost no risk of principal fluctuation. Generally, the longer a bond's maturity, the greater the risk and the greater the resulting yield. In today's high-interest-rate levels, however, short-term securities can be found with a 13-percent yield for six months. The catch is that you may not be able to reinvest your short-term funds continuously at such high rates. In the long run the 11½-percent bond yield is likely to average out higher than continued reinvestment in short-term securities. Despite appearances to the contrary, you should then get an extra reward for taking the risk of owning long-term bonds.

No one can say for sure what the returns on common stocks will be. But the stock market, as Oskar Morgenstern once observed, is like a gambling casino where the odds are rigged in favor of the players. Although stock prices do plummet, as they did so disastrously during the decade of the 1970s, the overall return of the past fifty years (including the 1970s) has been about 9 percent a year, including both dividends and capital gains. I believe that a portfolio of common stocks such as those that make up a typical mutual fund will earn 15 percent or more over the long term if you buy them at today's price levels. The actual yearly return can and probably will deviate substantially from target—in down years you could lose as much as 25 percent or more. Can you stand the sleepless nights in the bad years?

How about dreams in full color with quadraphonic sound? You might want to choose a portfolio of somewhat riskier (more volatile) stocks like those in aggressive growth-oriented mutual funds. These are the stocks in younger companies in newer technologies, where the promise of greater growth exists. Such companies are likely to be more volatile performers, and portfolios of these issues could easily lose half of their value in a bad market year. On the basis of current market conditions, however, your average rate of return could be in the neighborhood of 16–18 percent per year. Portfolios of riskier stocks have tended to outperform the market averages by small amounts. If you have no trouble sleeping during bear markets, and if you have the staying power to stick with your investments, an aggressive common stock portfolio may be just the right thing for you.

Real estate is a very tricky and often sleepless investment for most individuals. Nevertheless, the returns from real estate have been quite generous and similar to the returns from common stocks. I'll argue in Commandment VI that individuals who can afford to buy their own home are well advised to do so.

I realize that Table 7 slights gold, art objects, commodities, and many more exotic investment possibilities. Many of these have done very well over the past decade. Because of their substantial risk, and thus extreme volatility, it's impossible to describe them in terms similar to other investments; Commandment VII reviews them in greater detail. What is important here is to ask if their extreme risk suits your investment purposes.

In all likelihood, your sleeping point will be greatly influenced by the consequence of a loss to your financial survival. That is why the typical "widow" is often viewed in investment texts as unable to take on much risk. The widow has neither the life expectancy nor the ability to earn income outside her portfolio to be able to recoup losses. Any loss of capital and income will immediately affect her standard of living. At the other end of the spectrum is the "aggressive young businesswomen." She has both the life expectancy and sufficient earning power to maintain her standard of living in the face of any financial loss.

In addition, your psychological makeup will influence the degree of risk you are willing to assume. One investment advisor suggests that you consider what kind of Monopoly player you once were. Were you a plunger? Did you construct hotels on Boardwalk and Park Place? True, the other players seldom landed on your property, but when they did you could win the whole game in one fell swoop. Or did you prefer the steadier but moderate sources of income from the orange monopoly of St. James, Tennessee, and New York Avenues? The answers to these questions may give you some insight into your psychological makeup with respect to investing, and may help you choose the right categories of securities for you. Or perhaps the analogy breaks down when it comes to the money game, which is played for keeps. In any event, it is critical that you understand yourself before choosing specific securities for investment.

A second key investment step is to review how much of your investment return goes to Uncle Sam and your need for current income. Check your last year's income tax form (1040) and the taxable income you reported for the year. Table 8 shows the 1979 marginal tax brackets (rates paid on the last dollar of income) as well as the tax advantage of municipal (tax-exempt) bonds. If you are in a high tax bracket with little need for current income, you will prefer bonds that are tax exempt and stocks that have low dividend yields but promise favorably taxed long-term capital gains (where 60 percent of realized gains may be excluded from income and where taxes do not have to be paid until gains are realized, and perhaps never if the stocks are part of a bequest). On the other hand, if you are in a low tax bracket with high income needs for current consumption, you will be better off with taxable bonds and high-dividend-paying common stocks, so that you don't have to incur the heavy transactions charges involved in selling off shares periodically to meet current income needs. Remember also that the first $200 of dividend income is tax exempt for a couple filing a joint return. Thus, (almost) everybody should own enough stock to gain this tax-free income. A $2000 investment in AT&T with its almost 10-percent yield or a $4000 investment in IBM with its (approximate) 5-percent yield will produce tax-free income for a couple if that is their only holding.

These two steps—reviewing your risk level, and your tax bracket and income needs—seem obvious. But it is incredible how many people go astray by mismatching the types of securities they buy with their risk tolerances, and income and tax needs.

TABLE 8
The Tax-Free Edge of Municipal Bonds[a]
(for investors with differing taxable incomes—in thousands)

Single Return		$15–18		$18–23		$23–28		$28–34	$34–41		$41–55	
Joint Return	$20–24		$24–29		$29–35		$35–45		$45–60	$60–85		$85–109
% Tax Bracket	28	30	32	34	37	39	43	44	49	54	55	59

Tax-exempt yields — Equivalent Taxable Yields

Tax-exempt yields	28	30	32	34	37	39	43	44	49	54	55	59
6.00	8.33	8.57	8.82	9.09	9.52	9.84	10.53	10.71	11.76	13.04	13.33	14.63
7.00	9.72	10.00	10.29	10.61	11.11	11.48	12.28	12.50	13.73	15.22	15.56	17.07
8.00	11.11	11.43	11.76	12.12	12.70	13.11	14.04	14.29	15.68	17.39	17.78	19.51
9.00	12.50	12.88	13.24	13.64	14.29	14.75	15.79	16.07	17.65	19.57	20.00	21.95

SOURCE: Merrill Lynch, The Bond Book

[a]To see what a taxable-interest bond would have to yield to equal your take-home yield in a tax-free municipal bond, find your taxable-income bracket. Then find the yield in the left-hand column of a tax-free bond you might buy and read across until you find what percentage interest you would have to receive from a taxable security to equal that yield. For example, if your joint return income is $50,000, your marginal tax bracket is 49%. Thus, a 7.00% tax-free return is equal to a 13.73% taxable return. (Taxable income in thousands of dollars. Based on tax tables effective for 1979 income.)

The confusion of priorities so often displayed by investors is not unlike that exhibited by a young woman whose saga was recently written up in a London newspaper:

RED FACES IN PARK

London, Oct 30.

Secret lovers were locked in a midnight embrace when it all happened.

Wedged into a tiny two-seater sports car, the near-naked man was suddenly immobilised by a slipped disc, according to a doctor writing in a medical journal here.

Trapped beneath him his desperate girlfriend tried to summon help by sounding the hooter button with her foot. A doctor, ambulancemen, firemen and a group of interested passers-by quickly surrounded the couple's car in Regents Park.

Dr. Brian Richards of Kent said: "The lady found herself trapped beneath 200 pounds of a pain-racked, immobile man.

"To free the couple, firemen had to cut away the car frame," he added.

The distraught girl, helped out of the car and into a coat, sobbed: "How am I going to explain to my husband what has happened to his car?"

—Reuters.

Investors also are often torn between the same confusion of priorities. You can't seek safety of principal and then take a plunge with your investments into the riskiest of common stocks. You can't shelter your income from high marginal tax rates and then lock in returns of 11½ percent from taxable corporate bonds, no matter how attractive these investments may be. Yet, the annals of investment counselors are replete with stories of investors whose security holdings are inconsistent with their investment goals.

III. Render unto Caesar the Smallest Amount Possible

One of the best ways to obtain extra investment funds is to avoid taxes legally. We've already discussed tax-exempt bonds and the tax advantages of the first $100 of dividends and of long-term capital gains. But did you know that you pay no income taxes on money invested in retirement plans (or the earnings acquired from these investments) until you actually retire and use it? At that time you may be in a lower tax bracket—especially since the money you collect from Social Security is tax free. Even if you are not in a lower bracket, you will have paid no taxes on your retirement savings over the years. This commandment tells you how to reap these benefits.

First, check to see if your employer has a pension or profit-sharing plan. If so, you are home free. But what if your employer doesn't have such a plan? If you're single, you can contribute as much as 15 percent of your annual income up to $1500 a year to an Individual Retirement Account (IRA). If you're married and both you and your spouse work, you can contribute $3000. If your spouse is not working, you can contribute $1750. For self-employed people, Congress has created the Keogh plan. Self-employed individuals—from accountants to Avon ladies, barbers to real estate brokers, doctors to decorators—are all permitted to establish such a plan and contribute 15 percent of their income, up to $7500 annually. If you moonlight from your regular job, you can establish a Keogh on the income you earn on the side. Just as with the IRA, the money paid into Keogh plans is deductible from taxable income and the earnings are not taxed until they are withdrawn. If you qualify for either of these plans, you'll be making a big mistake not to take advantage of this perfectly legal way to checkmate the IRS and maximize your retirement savings to help you cope with the ravages of inflation.

Millions of taxpayers are currently overlooking what is one of the truly good deals around. Unless we look at a few numbers, it's impossible to realize what a difference these plans can make. Let's say you're 35 years old and contribute $1000 to an IRA or Keogh plan this year. Suppose you placed the plan in some fixed-income investments yielding 11 percent. In 30 years (at age 65) your $1000 investment would have compounded tax free to $24,-840.[1] Now suppose you withdrew the whole amount at age 65

[1]The calculation assumes you can continue to reinvest the interest earnings at the same 11-percent rate.

when you retire. If you were then in the 21-percent tax bracket you would retain $19,624 *after all taxes.* Consider now the alternative of not establishing a Keogh or IRA plan. Your $1000 would then be taxed at regular tax rates. If you are presently in the 32-percent bracket, that means you would retain only $680 for investment in 11-percent securities. What's more, each year's interest payments would be taxed so that your net earnings rate, after a tax of 32 percent, would only be 7.48 percent. At age 65 you would end up with only $6158 *after taxes,* assuming you didn't blow the money on a good toot sometime along the way. In this conservative example, an IRA or Keogh plan allows you to end up with over three times as much income after tax at retirement. And we've just looked at a single $1000 contribution; suppose you contributed $1000 every year, or better still, the maximum amount you could contribute to an IRA or Keogh. My advice is to save as much as you can through these tax-sheltered means. Use up any other savings you may have for current living expenses, if you must, so you can contribute the maximum allowed.

Is there a fly in the ointment? Yes, as the favorite expression of economists goes, "there ain't no such thing as a completely free lunch." You can't touch IRA or Keogh funds before turning fifty-nine and a half or becoming disabled. If you do, the amount withdrawn is taxed, and in addition you must pay a 10-percent penalty on it.

But even with this catch, I believe IRAs and Keoghs are still a good deal. While 10 percent of what you withdraw is indeed a stiff penalty, it's really not too much to pay for having been able to compound your savings tax free as well as to defer taxes on the income you put into the plan. Certainly, the advantages of staying in the plan for a few years would far outweigh the penalty even if you do withdraw some funds.

The important point is that if you plan to have any money saved up by the time you are fifty-nine and a half, you might as well do it in the form of tax-free retirement funds. Whatever savings and investment decisions you make, it's always better to make them tax free.

What can Keogh and IRA funds be invested in? You name it

—stocks, bonds, mutual funds, savings certificates, annuity contracts, and other investments. Your specific choice should depend on your risk preferences as well as the composition of your other investment holdings. You can choose from a wide variety of plans offered by savings institutions, securities dealers, insurance companies, and mutual funds. My own preference would be to use stock and bond funds under current market conditions, and I'll give you specific advice later on in choosing the best vehicle for you. You certainly don't want to invest in lower yielding tax-exempt securities, however, since your retirement fund will accumulate tax free anyway.

Any further questions regarding the plans? You can call your local office of the Internal Revenue Service for answers to specific questions. Also, the IRS puts out a publication, Number 590, 1980 edition, which goes over all the detailed regulations.

IV. Honor Thy Cash Reserves, That Their Yield May Compete with Inflation

It is well and good to say that in an era of inflation you shouldn't hold any monetary assets such as savings accounts since inflation erodes their real value. The problem is that we've already reviewed the necessity of holding some savings in a nest egg of ready assets for pending expenses such as college tuition, or for possible emergencies, or even for psychological support. Thus, individuals have a real dilemma. You know that if you put your money in a savings bank and get, say, 5½-percent interest at the end of a year during which the inflation rate is, say, 11 percent, you actually come out 5½ percent behind in terms of real purchasing power. In fact, the situation's even worse because the interest you get is subject to regular income taxes. It's not the bank's fault; they are not allowed by law to pay any more on these accounts, even if they wanted to. So what's a small saver to do?

The investor of substantial means has no problem. This investor can buy Treasury bills (short-term IOUs issued by the U.S. government) or bank CDs (short-term IOUs issued by banks, called certificates of deposit). But these instruments are issued in denominations of $10,000 to $25,000, respectively. If you have only a small amount of liquid assets, you can't get into this market directly. So how does the small saver avoid getting shafted? How do you get a rate of return that protects you against inflation? That is what this commandment is all about.

There are four short-term investment instruments that can at least help you stand up to inflation. These are: (1) money-market mutual funds; (2) six-month bank certificates; (3) money-market trusts; and (4) tax-exempt money-market funds.

Money-Market Mutual Funds ✓

In my judgment this is the best instrument for many investors' needs. It permits you to hedge against inflation even with your cash reserves. The money funds combine safety, high yields, and the right to withdraw money with no penalty attached. Available interest rates at the start of the 1980s are about 12–13 percent. These yields should allow you to keep even (at least before taxes) with the expected inflation rate for the months ahead. Most funds allow you to write large checks against the fund balance, generally in amounts of $500 or more. Interest earnings continue until the checks clear. These money funds are the best alternative to bank accounts and they have been extraordinarily popular. During 1979 alone, over $30 billion was put into these funds, leaving their year-end assets at over $40 billion dollars, four times as much as they were at the beginning of the year. A number of the available funds are described in Table 9.

These money funds invest in large bank certificates of deposit, commercial paper (short-term corporate IOUs), government securities, and other instruments. Since they pool the funds of many small investors, the money funds can buy larger issues beyond your financial reach. The funds sell for one dollar a share and aim to keep that principal constant. While there's no guarantee against a loss of principal, you shouldn't have trouble sleeping nights with the funds in Table 9. Even during the tough market period of 1979, these funds were able to keep the princi-

TABLE 9

Data on Selected Money-Market Funds

| Fund | Date originated | Minimum initial purchase | Minimum subsequent purchase | Total assets (in millions) | Current yield (1/1/80) | Distribution of portfolio holdings (percent) | | | | | | | |
						U.S. Treasury	U.S. Other	Repos[b]	Certificates of deposit	Banker's acceptances	Commercial paper	Eurocertificates of deposit	Other
Dreyfus Liquid Assets 600 Madison Avenue New York, NY 10022 800/223-5525	1974	2500	100	2157.8	12.8	2	—	3	39	11	19	26	—
Fidelity Cash Reserves 82 Devonshire Street Boston, MA 02109 800/225-6190	1979	1000	100	322.7	13.6	—	—	—	14	10	9	28	39
Intercapital Liquid Asset Fund, Inc. 1 Battery Park Plaza New York, NY 10004 800/221-2685	1975	5000	1000	2639.1	12.7	2	1	—	54	—	43	—	—

	Year											
Merrill Lynch Ready Assets 165 Broadway New York, NY 10080 800/221-7210 or call local office	1975	5000	1000	8131.0	12.4	8	6	5	59	15	7	—	—
The Reserve Fund, Inc. 810 Seventh Avenue New York, NY 10010 800/223-5547 800/223-9864	1970	1000	1000	1767.0	12.6	—	13	4	2	—	78	3
Whitehall Money Market Trust[a] P.O. Box 1100 Valley Forge, PA 19482 800/523-7910 (800/362-7688 in Pa.)	1974	3000	100	183.8	12.8	—	1	6	28	33	32	—	—

SOURCE: Donoghue's Money Fund Report. Current data on these funds can be obtained from Donoghue's service, P.O. Box 540, Holliston, MA 01746. Free sample copies of current reports are available on request.

[a]I am on the Board of Directors of this fund.

[b]Securities held under repurchase agreements.

pal value constant at a dollar, although in some cases this was accomplished only through not paying out all of the interest earnings of the fund for periods of several days. In judging the funds that are best for your sleeping scale you should know that the funds with longer average maturities and with riskier investments (such as Euro CDs, described below) will tend to offer somewhat higher returns as well as occasional dreams.

Six-Month Bank Certificates

Banks have fought back against this new competition with six-month $10,000 certificates with interest rates pegged to those available on Treasury bills of the same term to maturity. Usually they pay a bit less than the money funds, but these certificates are government insured up to $40,000 per buyer ($80,000 with your spouse). Thus, the certificates are even safer than the money funds and are an excellent medium for investors who can tie up their liquid funds for at least six months.

The certificates do have a number of disadvantages, however. First, you need to have a substantial nest egg—$10,000—before you can buy. Second, you can't write checks against the certificates as you can with the money funds. Most important, as in other aspects of life there is a substantial penalty for premature withdrawal. If you redeem your certificate in less than ninety days, you lose *all* interest. If you redeem after ninety days, you lose interest on the first ninety days and get paid interest only from the end of the ninety-day period until the time of redemption. Third, the yield on bank certificates is slightly less than that on six-month Treasury bills (also issued in $10,000 denominations) and is subject to state and local taxes (Treasury bills are exempt from these).

Money-Market Trusts

These are six-month certificates offered by brokerage firms. Unlike the money funds, which are continuously managed, the trusts simply buy a package of high-yielding instruments with a maturity of six-months and then liquidate the trust at the end of the investment period. The major advantage of these trusts is that they offer individual investors with as little as $1000 to invest the highest available short-term yields. One trust offered at the end of 1979 yielded well over 13 percent.

How do the trusts do it? A careful reading of Chapter 2 will suggest the answer. They take on more risk. Basically, the trusts invest in so-called Eurodollar CDs. A Eurodollar is a dollar on deposit outside the United States, and these certificates, even when issued by foreign branches of U.S. banks, are not subject to the same regulations as dollars on deposit within the U.S. A foreign government could impose restrictions on foreign branches of U.S. banks. For example, they could impose exchange controls that would block payment of the interest and principal on these certificates. However unlikely such an event may be, these investments do entail some additional risk. Is the extra interest, as much as one percentage point, worth it? Go back to Commandment II—Know Thyself—for the answer. It depends on your potential liquidity needs and your psychological makeup. Remember also that the six-month trusts do involve some penalty for early withdrawal, although not as severe as for the bank certificates. Also, if you plan to be invested for a considerable period of time, you should realize that there is a risk that you will not be able to reinvest your funds at the same high rates available at the start of 1980.

Tax-Exempt Money-Market Funds

This instrument may be useful for some investors, particularly those who pay marginal tax rates of at least 50 percent. A disadvantage with all the previous vehicles is that the interest is fully taxable. Investors in very high brackets will find that, after taxes, even the highest of the yields offered will not compensate for inflation. This led to the establishment of the first tax-exempt money-market fund, the Warwick Municipal Bond Fund short-term portfolio.

Warwick invests in a portfolio of short-term high-quality tax-exempt issues. It thus produces daily tax-exempt income and a history of high capital stability. As do the regular money-market funds, it provides instant liquidity and free checking for your large bills ($500 or more). The minimum investment required is $3000. As of the end of 1979, the fund was yielding about 5.3%. Those in the highest tax brackets will find this yield more attractive than the after-tax yield of the regular money funds.[2] Unfortunately, however, the existence of taxes makes it impossible for such investors to hedge fully against inflation with any short-term funds.

V. Thou Shalt Not Bear False Witness Against Bonds

Let's face it, bonds have been a lousy place to put your money for at least the past two decades. Inflation has eaten away at the real value of the bonds with a vengeance. For example, the U.S. Savings Bond you bought for $18.75 five years ago will now fetch $25 when you redeem it. The trouble is that while the $18.75 invested in such a bond five years ago may have filled your gas tank twice, the $25 cashed in today does little more than fill it once, if you can find a station whose pumps aren't dry. In fact, your real return has been negative, as inflation has eroded the purchasing power of your dollars at a faster rate than your interest earnings were compounding. Small wonder many investors view the bond as an unmentionable four-letter word.

In fact, the U.S. Savings Bond program, with its touching appeals to patriotism and good citizenship, is a monumental ripoff. At the start of 1980, the new improved Series EE Savings Bonds paid interest at only 6½ percent when held to maturity in eleven years. This rate is not only far below the current inflation rate, but also is not much more than half what the government is paying on regular bonds sold on the open market. I find it incon-

[2]You can get an application and prospectus by writing to P.O. Box 1100, Valley Forge, PA 19482, or by calling 800/523-7910 (800/362-7688 in Pennsylvania). Again, I must alert the reader that I serve on the board of this fund.

ceivable that our government continues to deceive its own citizens in this way. While the bonds have some tax advantages, they are simply not competitive with other instruments available. Be unpatriotic—avoid Series EE and HH bonds completely.

Of course, other bonds have also been poor investments in recent years as the interest rates they carried often proved insufficient to offer adequate inflation protection. Investors simply did not realize ten to twenty years ago the amount of inflation to come. But remember Chapter 2: markets are reasonably efficient and investors now refuse to buy bonds until their yields are sufficient to offer a reasonable degree of compensation for the expected loss in the dollar's purchasing power. Thus, good-quality long-term bonds at the start of the 1980s were yielding 11–12 percent in the open market. This yield freely translates into protection against long-term inflation of 8–9 percent and a real rate of return above that inflation of about 3 percent. Of course, it is always possible that the actual long-run rate of inflation may be considerably greater than the 8- to 9-percent inflation premium implicit in current bond yields. But the point is that bonds do offer a degree of inflation protection and their current high yields and relative stability do make them a suitable investment for many investors.

I have three specific suggestions you may want to consider: (1) the floating-rate note (a bond with particularly good principal stability since its interest rate floats each half year with the current level of interest rates); (2) the closed-end bond fund (a way of locking in today's high yields on corporate bonds for a long period of time, while purchasing diversified portfolios of bonds at discounts around 15 percent from their market values); and (3) tax-exempt bonds (for those who are fortunate enough to be in high tax brackets).

Have No Fear of Floating

One of the most interesting financial innovations of the 1970s, floating-rate notes provide the closest thing we have to inflation indexing in the financial markets. This is done through a contract interest rate that automatically changes each half year in line with the market yields of U.S. Treasury bills. The premise is that, by and large, Treasury bill yields will rise and fall with inflation rates. (The economic evidence suggests that this is in fact the case.) Toward the end of 1979, Treasury bills were yielding about 12 percent, a bit higher than most forecasts of the inflation rate for 1980. The hedge is far from perfect (and often Treasury bill yields are below the inflation rate), but at least these floaters provide investors with an instrument whose yield will tend to vary with the rate of inflation.

Floating-rate notes have several features that may make them an attractive investment for you. First, as noted above, the semiannual interest payment floats with the Treasury bill rate, e.g., 1 percent above the bill yield. Second, there is usually a minimum interest rate set (e.g., 7.50 percent in one recent issue) no matter how low Treasury bill yields fall. Third, the issues are often convertible into long-term bonds at the option of the holder, but at rates somewhat below competitive long-term yields. Finally, the floaters are available in denominations of $1000. These features imply a considerable degree of capital stability for the floaters. Normal bonds (with fixed-interest payments) fall in price as market yields rise so as to provide new purchasers of the bonds yields that are competitive with the higher level of rates. Floaters issued with generous terms will remain fairly stable in price, however, since their contract interest rate gets adjusted semiannually.

Some of the earlier floating-rate notes did not have terms that were as generous as those on more recent issues, nor did they offer rates of return for large investors that were as great as could be obtained by holding bank certificates of deposit directly. Thus, the early floaters tended to decline in price until their yields were competitive with those available in the open market.

Table 10 shows the current prices and yields of a representative sample of early issues. At the going market prices, these issues should provide good returns and excellent capital stability from here on out. Either these issues or more recent floaters, which now offer better premiums over Treasury bill yields, will

TABLE 10
Recent Issues of Floating-Rate Notes

Issue and maturity	Coupon when issued	Start of 1980		
		Interest coupon	Price	Current yield(%)
Citicorp, 2004	11.05	12.70	95¼	13.4
Chemical New York Corp., 2004	10.90	12.65	94¾	13.4
Republic of Texas, 2004	11.05	12.65	95	13.3
Chase Manhattan, 2009	10.75	12.25	92¼	13.3

serve investors in low tax brackets very well. For that portion of their portfolio in stable assets, the floaters will provide an excellent measure of inflation protection.

Closed-End Bond Funds Can Be a Good Deal

If interest rates and the inflation rate retreat from recent double-digit levels in the 1980s, it will turn out to have been a better strategy to buy regular long-term bonds rather than the new floaters. The long-term bond strategy will allow you to lock in today's high yields for many years into the future. Moreover, your bonds will tend to rise in price as eager buyers will bid up the prices of bonds promising high contractual interest payments. The best way to buy long-term bonds is through a publicly traded closed-end bond fund, which holds a diversified portfolio of high-quality bonds.

I'm going to explain the whole concept of closed-end funds in considerable detail in Chapter 5. For now, a few basic facts are necessary. Unlike open-end bond funds, whose shares are issued in unlimited quantities and who stand ready to redeem their shares at net asset value, the closed-end funds have only a specific finite number of shares outstanding and they trade in the market for whatever price investors will pay. The shares of the funds are nearly all traded on the New York Stock Exchange. Mainly because of general investor discontent with Wall Street, the shares of some bond funds have recently been trading at discounts of 15 percent from the market value of the bonds they hold. Thus, you are able to buy bonds at eighty-five cents on the dollar. This allows you to get an even higher yield than if you bought the underlying bonds directly.

At present discounts of 15 percent (or more), the funds are an excellent buy. You should keep in mind, however, that such funds charge yearly expenses amounting to close to 1 percent of the value of the fund. Consequently, you need a discount of nearly 10 percent before you'd do as well with the funds as you would on your own. Let's see why. Suppose bonds were yielding about 10 percent per year. If you bought directly you would earn $10 for every $100 you put in. The bond fund deducts $1 (1 percent) in expenses, however, and distributes only $9 per $100 of asset value. Thus, you have to buy at a 10-percent discount, i.e., at $90, to earn a 10-percent return. On the other hand, if you can buy at greater than a 10-percent discount, you'll do better through a closed-end bond fund than you could do on your own. Also there is, of course, some value to the convenience of the bond fund as well as to the diversification it offers.

The Appendix to this chapter presents a listing of closed-end bond funds, with information about them and their investment policies. If the portfolio contains lower grade bonds, private placements, bonds with equity features, and if it is leveraged (if it buys some of its securities on margin), you can expect a much riskier (less stable) performance as well as some extra long-run return. Information is also given about the fund's policy with respect to portfolio turnover. More turnover means that the fund does a good deal of in-and-out trading, and you know how the efficient-market theorists feel about that. More up-to-date information about the funds can be found in the weekly listings in your newspaper and in the most recent edition of Wiesenberger's *Investment Companies.*

Some of the closed-end bond funds available offer the investor a portfolio of securities partway between a regular equity and a standard bond portfolio. These are the funds that invest in so-called convertible securities such as convertible bonds. A convertible bond is like a regular IOU except that it is also convertible into common stock at the option of the holder. If the company's stock goes up, it usually becomes worthwhile to convert, so convertibles have important equity features.

Convertibles have been called "topless but not bottomless wonders." They are topless because, unlike regular bonds where your payoff is fixed no matter how well the company does, "converts" generally go up in price as the company prospers and its common stock advances. On the other hand, should the company fall on hard times, the stability of a fixed and prior-claim bond will generally put a floor on the value of the convertible bond, unless the company gets in so much trouble that it goes straight down the tube. Because of this advantage, the yield rate on convertibles is generally well below the going yields on similar securities without the convertibility feature.

Tax-Exempt Bonds Are Useful for High-Bracket Investors

If you are in a very high tax bracket, neither floaters nor closed-end bond funds are right for you. You need the tax-exempt bonds issued by state and local governments and by various governmental authorities, such as port authorities or toll roads. The interest from these bonds doesn't even have to be reported on your tax form, and bonds from the state in which you live are typically exempt from any state income taxes.

This tax exemption gives a subsidy to state and local governments since they can issue bonds at lower interest rates than if the bonds were fully taxable. Economists have argued that it's an inefficient subsidy (it would be cheaper, so this argument goes, for the U.S. Treasury just to pay the state and local governments to issue taxable bonds). But since that's the present law there is no reason why you shouldn't take advantage of it.

By now, if you've carefully read my commandment II, Know Thyself, you know whether municipal bonds are compatible with your tax bracket and income needs. Right now, medium-quality long-term corporate bonds are yielding around 11½ percent and tax-exempt issues of comparable quality yield about 8¼ percent. Suppose you are in the 40-percent tax bracket. By this I mean the rate at which your last dollar of income was taxed—not your average rate. Table 11 shows that after-tax income is $135 higher on the tax-exempt security, and is clearly the better investment in your tax bracket. Even in the 32-percent tax bracket, tax-exempts might pay depending on the exact yields available in the market when you make your purchase.

Look carefully at new long-term revenue bond issues of various public authorities such as port authorities, established turnpikes, power authorities, etc. These bonds (called term bonds) often provide very attractive tax-exempt investment vehicles. I would suggest that you buy new issues rather than already outstanding securities, because new-issue yields are usually a bit sweeter than the yields of "seasoned outstanding bonds." I also suggest that you stick with issues rated at least A by Moody's and Standard & Poor's rating services to keep your risk within reasonable bounds. These term bond issues usually mature in thirty years or more, but they often enjoy a good trading market after they have been issued. Thus, if you want to sell the bonds later you can do so with reasonable ease, particularly if you own at least $5000 worth of a single issue.

TABLE 11
Tax-Exempt vs. Taxable Bonds

Type of bond	Interest paid	Applicable taxes (40% rate)	After-tax income
8¼% tax-exempt	$ 825	$ 0	$825
11½% taxable	1150	460	690

Avoid serial bonds. These are tax-exempt bonds that mature serially over perhaps thirty different years or more. These issues are usually tougher to sell than term bonds if you have to raise funds prior to maturity. Also, yields on serial issues (especially the shorter term ones) usually tend to be lower than on term bonds, in part because they are particularly attractive to institutions like banks that pay taxes at high corporate rates. Unless you have funds to invest for some specific period of time and want to match the maturity of the bond you buy with the timing of your fund requirements, these bonds are best left to institutional buyers. So ask your broker how the "new-issue calendar" looks. By waiting a week or so until a new high-yielding revenue term bond comes out, you may be able to improve your interest return substantially.

There is one nasty "heads I win, tails you lose" feature of bonds that you should know about. If interest rates go up, the price of your bonds will go down, as I noted earlier. But if interest rates go down, the issuer can often "call" the bonds away from you (repay the debt early) and then issue new bonds at lower rates.

To protect yourself, make sure your bonds have a call-protection provision that prevents the issuer from calling your bonds to refund them at lower rates. Many tax-exempt revenue issues offer about ten years of call protection. After that the bonds are callable, but typically at a premium over what you paid for them. Make sure to ask about call protection, especially during periods when interest rates are higher than usual, as they are at the start of the 1980s.

There are tax-exempt bond funds—but no closed-end ones—available at good discounts. If you have substantial funds to invest in tax-exempts ($25,000 or more), I see little reason for you to choose a fund for your tax-exempt purchases and pay the management fees involved. If you have followed the previous rules and confined your purchases to high-quality bonds, there is little need for you to diversify among many different securities. You'll get more interest return if you do it yourself and invest directly. On the other hand, if you have just a few thousand to invest, you will find it costly to buy and sell small lots of bonds, and a fund will provide convenient liquidity and diversification for you.

VI. Thou Shalt Own Thine Own Home—and Perhaps Covet Thy Neighbor's

There's no place like home, especially when inflation is raging all about you. Remember Scarlett O'Hara? She was broke at the end of the Civil War, but she still had her beloved plantation, Tara. A good house and land keeps its value no matter what happens to money. As long as the world's population continues to grow, the demand for real estate will be among the most dependable inflation hedges available. Those of you who do own your own homes will probably find that the house you live in is the best investment you ever made in your life.

One hundred years ago, Henry George sounded the call for real estate investment:

Go, get yourself a piece of ground, and hold possession. . . . You need do nothing more. You may sit down and smoke your pipe; you may lie around like the lazzaroni of Naples or the leperos of Mexico; you may go up in a balloon, or down a hole in the ground and without doing one stroke of work, without adding one iota to the wealth of the community, in ten years you will be rich.

By and large, George's advice turned out to be pretty good.

Although the calculation is tricky, it appears that the returns to real estate have been quite generous. Real estate returns appear to be roughly comparable to the long-run returns from common stocks. Not only that, they appear to be less variable from year to year and thus more predictable than stock returns. But the market is less efficient than the stock market. There may be hundreds of knowledgable investors who study the worth of every common stock. Perhaps only a handful of prospective buyers assess the worth of a particular real estate property. Thus, the market is one where individual pieces of property are not always appropriately priced. Finally, real estate returns seem to be higher than stock returns during periods when inflation is accelerating but do less well during periods of disinflation. In sum, real estate has proved itself to be a good investment providing generous returns and excellent inflation-hedge characteristics.

The natural real estate investment for most people is the single-family home or condominium. You have to live somewhere, and buying has several tax advantages over renting. Because Congress wanted to encourage home ownership and the values associated with this, it gave the homeowner a number of tax breaks: (1) while rent is not deductible from income taxes, the two major expenses associated with home ownership—interest payments on your mortgage and property taxes—are fully deductible; (2) any realized gains in the value of your house are taxed at favorable capital-gains rates (if you have owned the house for over a year); (3) if you buy another, more expensive house, you can defer realizing a capital gain; and (4) if you sell your home after age fifty-five, $100,000 of the gains are tax exempt. In addition, houses are a good vehicle to force you to save, and they provide enormous emotional satisfaction. My advice is, "Own your own home if you can possibly afford it."

Once you find a successful investment, why not repeat it? For example, rent from another well-located, well-maintained single-family house or condominium can provide generous returns—especially if you know the property well. If you have the temperament to accept a 2:00 A.M. call from your neighbor complaining that the furnace doesn't work, you might even adore the house next door and purchase it as a rental property. You're likely to have the best knowledge of the market and the specific characteristics of the property in your own neighborhood. If the rent just covers your interest and taxes, you can come out well ahead. The depreciation of the house provides good tax writeoffs, and any rise in the value of the house will be taxed at favorable capital-gains rates.

Despite the recent rash of fabulous get-rich-quick stories about real estate investing, there are risks aplenty. A few deserve special mention. There is a maxim in the real estate field that there are three principles of real estate investment: location, location, and location. And location is a fickle thing. A country home without access to public transportation is no longer as desirable as it was in the early 1970s. Now that family size is shrinking, six- and seven-bedroom homes are no longer de rigeur. There is another real estate maxim that "the buyer needs 100 eyes, the seller not one." As mentioned above, the market can be inefficient and not appropriately priced. Another risk is the sharp recent rise in real estate prices in the late 1970s—especially the speculative fever in certain areas. It's well to remember the lessons of Chapter 1's discussion of the "greater fool" theory. Some cooling off of prices in 1980 would be needed to create really attractive opportunities. And keep in mind that by the mid-1980s the very favorable demographic trends which have helped inflate house prices will begin to diminish as the growth in household formation slows considerably. There are also particular risks in specific real estate investments. For example, local restrictions can prevent you from building on an investment in land. Rent controls can turn a profitable apartment house investment into a sour lemon, especially since property taxes go on whether you can rent on favorable terms or not. It's also important to remember that real estate cannot be sold quickly or inexpensively. It's also very difficult for an investor to obtain adequate diversification in real estate since each unit typically involves a great deal of money.[3] Finally, the greatest risk facing real estate investment is the risk of disinflation. If the inflation rate in the 1980s were to fall sharply from recent levels, real estate is likely to produce far inferior returns to stocks and bonds.

Despite the risks, well-located real estate, which is not excessively priced, remains a useful investment medium—capable of

[3]There are some Real Estate Investment Trusts (REITs) around that work on the same principle as a closed-end fund and allow the investor to buy a diversified portfolio of holdings, often at a discount from book value. In principle I like these investments. Many of these trusts invest in mortgages rather than ownership interests in real estate, however. Moreover, it is very difficult even for professionals (let alone individual investors) to evaluate these instruments.

producing generous returns and providing an excellent inflation hedge. Every investing household should plan to own its own home.

VII. Thou Shalt Not Bow Down to Gold or Other "Things"

The period at the beginning of the 1980s might well go down in investment history as the age of gold. Neither time nor government action could stem the rise of the metal's price. And gold appeared to cast a glow over other sterile, non-dividend-paying investments: diamonds, other metals such as copper and silver, and collectibles such as art, rugs, and porcelains all became popular investment vehicles.

Publishers jumped on this golden bandwagon and a number of "how-to-beat-inflation" books came out touting investments in "things" rather than in paper securities. The premise was that you and everybody else consumes "things" and if you want to preserve real purchasing power, then you can do so by owning specific commodities. For example, if you eat TV dinners and drive Volkswagen Rabbits, the way to preserve real purchasing power is to store away TV dinners and VW Rabbits. There's something to this advice. Indeed, in countries such as Brazil, which have suffered from hyperinflation, one can often see VW Rabbits up on blocks in the backyards of middle-class neighborhoods, for this is the way people hedge their savings against inflation.

The problem is that "things" often don't yield a stream of benefits such as dividend returns. Moreover, they can be costly to store and protect. They can even spoil. The VW Rabbit in your backyard can rust and the three-year-old TV dinner in your freezer may not taste very good. While agreeing with the notion of owning real assets, I prefer the kind of assets that produce a return while they are giving you inflation protection. That's why I like real estate and common stocks.

Still, there's no denying that for those who feed on economic

"I'm putting all my money into 'things.'"

Drawing by Geo. Price. © 1979 The New Yorker Magazine, Inc.

paranoia, the gold rush of 1979 was a banner year. People who early in the year pooh-poohed gold at a price of less than $300 an ounce, swallowed awfully hard when they saw it rise to more than $600 an ounce. At the start of the 1980s gold continued to soar—approaching the $1000-an-ounce mark. The doomsday groupies on the other hand were ecstatic, having long recommended a portfolio consisting entirely of gold. The price of gold feeds on anxiety and we certainly have had much cause for worry.

The problem is that gold is a sterile investment in a rational world. It does not yield dividends and can be costly to store and protect. Moreover, the sharp run-up in prices in 1979–80 is uncomfortably close in my mind to the tulip-bulb craze reported in Chapter 1. I am not panning gold for all time. Gold can be a useful investment to reduce risks because gold prices generally move counter to trends in the U.S. market. Moreover, anything can happen when it's tulip time in the market. If gold can sell at $900 an ounce, it can just as easily sell for $1800 an ounce (or $450 an ounce). But buying gold *at today's prices* is simply not in my judgment a rational investment decision. And I've noticed that even some of its staunchest supporters are beginning to say that gold is in for rough times.

Diamonds are also everybody's best friend these days. Again, there are enormous risks and disadvantages for individual investors. One must remember that there are large commission costs in buying diamonds. Not only that, there are fads in the way diamonds are cut. Despite assurances to the contrary, you will seldom be able to buy at true wholesale prices. It's also extraordinarily hard for an individual to judge quality and I can assure you the number of telephone calls you get from folks wishing to sell diamonds will greatly exceed the calls from those who want to buy them.

Another popular current investment strategy is investment in "collectibles." There are thousands of salesmen around touting everything from Renoir to rugs, Tiffany lamps to rare stamps, art deco to airsick bags. I think there's nothing wrong in buying "things" you can love—and God knows people do have strange tastes—but my advice is buy those things because you love them, not because you expect them to appreciate in value. Contrary to popular belief, the inflation-adjusted value of art objects and collectibles does not generally increase. There are also enormous commissions when you buy and sell. Suppose you bought some collectibles from a dealer for $1000; the dealer keeps 50 percent which, after sales tax and various charges, leaves $400 for the original seller. Suppose in five years the market value increases to four times what the seller got, from $400 to $1600. Now suppose you sell your collectibles at auction. The auction house might take its commission of $350 and send you a check for $1250. In this scenario then, you've made a profit of 25 percent in five years, less than the rate of inflation, and all this supposed that your collectibles appreciated to an astronomical 400 percent of their original value—certainly an unlikely event.

Ask yourself why everyone is so willing to part with things whose value is supposedly increasing. And don't forget that fakes and forgeries are common. A portfolio of collectibles also often implies hefty insurance premiums, endless maintenance charges, and the absence of dividends or interest. To make money collecting, you need great originality and taste. You must buy first-class objects when no one else wants them, not inferior schlock when a vast uninformed public enthusiastically bids them up. I think that most people who think they are collecting profit are really collecting trouble.

Two other popular instruments these days are commodities and stock options. In addition to gold, you can buy contracts for the delivery of a variety of commodities from grains to metals. It's a fast market where professionals can benefit greatly but where individuals who don't know what they are doing can easily get clobbered. Similarly, stock options can provide investors with a variety of risk-enhancing as well as risk-reducing strategies. But again, it's a highly complex market and I fear that most individual investors who are not highly trained in the evaluation of options contracts will make much money for their brokers but little, if any, for themselves. My advice to the nonprofessional investor: Don't go against the grain and don't exercise all your options.

One last reminder! Suppose gold continues to rise and sells at the astronomical price of $3000 an ounce in December 1990. Based on a purchase at its January 1980 price, the total return you will receive will actually be less than that provided by an 11½-percent bond.

VIII. Thou Shalt Take Stocks unto Thyself and Treasure Them Above All Others

Common stocks represent ownership claims on real things—factories, inventories, machine tools, and assembly lines. But unlike collectibles, the assets behind common stocks produce a stream of future returns. These returns can either be paid out in dividends or reinvested to produce even larger dividends in the future. Moreover, common stocks are available at the best dividend yields and the lowest prices relative to the assets behind them in years. The major message of this book is: "Make common stocks the cornerstone of your portfolio." They are the best inflation hedge for the 1980s. Given the market's disastrous performance over the past decade, how can an honest person make such a recommendation? That's a long story, long enough for a chapter all to itself, and I hope to make a true stock believer out of you once you've read Chapter 4. But before you convert, don't forget my last investment commandments.

IX. Eschew the Money Changers at the Temple: Buy Your Stocks at Wholesale

Even though markets may be reasonably efficient so that investment managers cannot pick portfolios that beat the broad stock averages, there is a way to assure yourself of better than average returns. Diversified portfolios of common stocks like IBM and AT&T are currently available at large discounts from their market prices. Why pay full price when you can buy at a discount that goes as high as 30 percent? The vehicle through which these bargains are available is the closed-end investment company. These closed-end stock funds are similar to the closed-end bond funds described above. Because I think this recommendation is so important, I will spend a good deal of Chapter Five discussing the strategy in detail and giving you rules to follow so that you can choose the specific investments that are right for you.

You can buy your brokerage services at wholesale prices as well. There are a number of brokers around today who will execute your stock orders at discounts that range up to 75 percent from the standard commission rates charged by the leading brokerage houses. The discount broker provides a plain pipe-rack service. If you want your hand held, if you want opinions and investment suggestions, if you want a broker you can call for quotations and other information, the discount broker is *not* for you. If, however, you know exactly what you want to buy, the discount broker can get it for you at much lower commission rates than the standard full-service house. If after reading Chapter 5 you decide to buy some of the closed-end funds I recommend, the discount broker offers you a way to buy them at double discounts—at discounts from market prices and at discount commission rates.

It's not too hard to find discount brokers. Just read the financial pages of your daily or Sunday paper and you'll find their ads with such catchy titles as "Full commissions are for the herds" and "There's nothing discount about [our service] except [our] commission rates." For pure execution of stock market orders you can use a discounter with complete confidence. The discounters all belong to the Security Investors Protection Corporation, which insures all accounts up to $100,000.

X. Thou Shalt Diversify

There's an old biblical proverb that "in the multitude of counselors there is safety." The same can be said of investments. Diversification reduces risk and makes it far more likely that you will achieve the kind of good average long-run return that meets your investment objective. The theory behind the diversification principle is the old saw that you shouldn't put all your eggs into one basket. But since we're talking about stocks that cost a lot more than eggs, it would be worth your time to review the following illustration.

Let's suppose we have a tropical island economy with only two businesses. The first is a large resort, the second an umbrella manufacturer. Weather affects the fortunes of both. During sunny seasons the resort does a booming business and umbrella sales plummet. During rainy seasons, tourists stay home and the umbrella manufacturer enjoys high sales and large profits. Table 12 shows some hypothetical returns for the two businesses dur-

TABLE 12
The Advantages of Diversification

Weather	Umbrella manufacturer	Resort owner
Rainy season	50%	−25%
Sunny season	−25%	50%

ing the different seasons. If one-half the seasons were sunny and one-half rainy, an investor in the umbrella manufacturer would earn an average return of 12½ percent: half the time earning a 50-percent return and half the time losing 25 percent. Investment in the resort would produce the same results. Investing in either one of these businesses would be fairly risky, however, because there could be several sunny or rainy seasons in a row.

Suppose, however, that the investor diversified and put half his money in the umbrella manufacturer's and half in the resort owner's businesses. In sunny seasons, a one-dollar investment in the resort would produce a fifty-cent return, while a one-dollar investment in the umbrella manufacturer would lose twenty-five cents. The investor's total return would be twenty-five cents (fifty cents minus twenty-five cents), which is 12½ percent of his total investment of two dollars.

Note that during rainy seasons exactly the same thing happens —only the names are changed. Investment in the umbrella manufacturer produces a good 50-percent return while the investment in the resort loses 25 percent. Again, however, the diversified investor makes a 12½-percent return on his total investment.

This simple illustration points out the basic advantage of diversification. An investor is sure of making a 12½-percent return each year no matter what happens to the weather. The trick that made the game work was that while both companies were risky (returns were variable from year to year), the companies had opposite reactions to weather conditions. As long as there is some lack of parallelism in the fortunes of the individual companies in the economy, diversification will always reduce risk. In the present case, where there is a perfect negative relationship between the companies' fortunes (one always does well when the other does poorly), diversification can totally eliminate risk.

The rub is that, in fact, the fortunes of most companies move pretty much in tandem. When there is a recession and people are unemployed, they may buy neither summer vacations nor umbrellas. Therefore, one should not expect in practice to get the neat kind of total risk elimination just shown. Nevertheless, since company fortunes don't always move completely in parallel, investment in a diversified portfolio of stocks is likely to be less risky than investment in one or two single securities.

It is easy to carry the lessons of this illustration to actual portfolio construction. Suppose you were considering combining General Motors and its major supplier of new tires in a stock portfolio. Would diversification be likely to give you much risk reduction? Probably not. If General Motors's sales slump, GM will be buying fewer new tires from the tire manufacturer. In general, diversification will not help much if there is a high degree of parallelism between the fortunes of the two companies.

On the other hand, if General Motors were combined with a government contractor in a depressed area, diversification might reduce risk substantially. It usually has been true that as the nation goes, so goes General Motors. If consumer spending is down (or if an oil crisis comes close to paralyzing the nation), General Motors's sales and earnings are likely to be down and the nation's level of unemployment up. Now, if the government makes a habit during times of high unemployment of giving out contracts to the depressed area (to alleviate some of the unemployment miseries there), it could well be that the returns of General Motors and those of the contractor do not move in phase. The two stocks might even tend to move in opposite directions.

The example may seem a bit strained, and most investors will realize that when the market gets clobbered just about all stocks go down. Still, at least at certain times, some stocks do move against the market. Gold stocks are often given as one example, and foreign stock markets may not always move in the same direction as our own. The point to realize in setting up a portfolio is that while the variability of the returns from individual stocks is important, even more important in judging the risk of a portfolio is the extent to which the securities move in parallel.

True diversification depends on having stocks in your portfolio that are not all dependent on the same economic variables (consumer spending, business investment, housing construction, etc.). Wise investors will diversify their portfolios not by names or industries but by the determinants that influence the fluctuations of various securities.

With this diversification principle in mind, it is easy to fit the ten commandments of this chapter together. While I strongly recommend common stocks as the cornerstone—even the whole foundation—of your investment strategy, they should not comprise the whole structure of your assets. The various bond-type assets such as floating-rate notes should be very helpful in reducing overall risk because their returns will not move completely in parallel with stock returns. Indeed, at times the returns from floating-rate notes will decline just when stock prices are going up and producing especially generous returns. Similarly, real estate returns will not always tend to move together with common stock returns. Even gold, if appropriately priced, could play a role in risk reduction since it has tended to move in opposite directions to U.S. stock returns. So don't limit your investments to any one area. The investor who's wise, diversifies.

Appendix: Information on Closed-End Bond Funds

TABLE 13
Information on Closed-End Bond Funds

Fund	Exchange traded	Year begun	Price (10/79)	Net asset value (10/79)	Discount (10/79)	Percent dividend yield (est. by Standard & Poor's)	1978 Expense ratio (% of net assets)	Average discount (six years through 1979)[a]
American General Bond Fund, Inc.	NYSE	1970	20¾	21.63	4.1	10.7	0.71	2.2 (P)
Bunker Hill Income Securities, Inc.	NYSE	1973	17⅞	20.30	12.0	11.6	0.84	6.2
Circle Income Shares, Inc.	OTC	1973	12⅜	13.36	7.4	10.0	0.29	2.4 (P)
CNA Income Shares, Inc.	NYSE	1973	10½	12.18	16.9	11.3	0.84	10.5
Current Income Shares, Inc.	OTC	1973	10⅛	11.75	13.8	11.7	0.80	10.0
Drexel Bond-Debenture Trading Fund	NYSE	1971	15⅞	18.81	15.6	10.8	1.18	16.0
Excelsior Income Shares, Inc.	NYSE	1973	16⅝	19.88	16.4	11.2	0.78	12.0
Federated Income and Private Placement	OTC	1972	8⅞	9.58	7.4	12.4	1.30	5.3
Fort Dearborn Income Securities, Inc.	NYSE	1972	12⅜	14.12	12.4	11.1	0.71	9.7
Hattaras Income Securities, Inc.	NYSE	1973	14¼	16.78	15.1	11.4	0.80	4.6
INA Investment Securities, Inc.	NYSE	1973	15½	19.07	18.7	11.6	1.07	14.5
Independence Square Income Securities, Inc.	OTC	1972	16⅛	19.10	15.6	11.1	0.88	0.3 (P)

Intercapital Income Securities, Inc.	NYSE	1973	18⅝	20.54	9.3	11.8	0.68	1.2 (P)
John Hancock Investors, Inc.	NYSE	1973	17⅞	NA	14.3	11.7	0.65	6.8
John Hancock Income Securities, Corp.	NYSE	1971	14⅜	16.24	11.5	11.7	0.62	7.4
Mass. Mutual Income Investors, Inc.	NYSE	1972	10⅜	12.18	14.8	11.6	0.84	12.8
Montgomery Street Income Securities	NYSE	1973	18⅝	20.57	9.7	11.4	0.65	4.8
Mutual of Omaha Interest Shares, Inc.	NYSE	1972	12⅞	14.87	13.4	11.7	0.69	9.5
Pacific American Income Shares, Inc.	NYSE	1973	12	14.42	16.8	11.8	0.72	12.4
St. Paul Securities Income, Inc.	NYSE	1972	10	11.44	12.6	11.0	0.82	9.6
State Mutual Securities, Inc.	NYSE	1973	9¾	11.94	18.3	11.2	0.94	12.7
Transamerica Income Shares, Inc.	NYSE	1972	19⅞	21.57	7.9	11.4	0.65	8.4
U.S. Life Income Fund, Inc.	NYSE	1972	9½	11.02	13.8	12.2	1.74	0.9
Vestaur Securities, Inc.	NYSE	1972	11¾	12.69	7.4	12.5	1.00	2.3

SOURCE: Wiesenberger Investment Services and *Wall Street Journal*.

[a](P) = premium.

TABLE 14

Closed-End Bond Funds' Investment Policies

Fund	Investment policy
American General Bond Fund, Inc.	Diversified; 80% high-grade debt securities, 20% other bonds with no equity features; up to 20% private placements.
Bunker Hill Income Securities, Inc.	Diversified; 75% high-grade debt securities, 25% other bonds, some with equity features and preferred stocks, with no more than 10% in restricted securities and non-Canadian foreign issues. Approximate turnover rate 75% and leverage up to 33% total assets.
Circle Income Shares, Inc.	Diversified; 75% high-grade debt securities, up to 25% in securities with equity features, preferred and common stock. 20% in privately placed, restricted securities, and leverage up to 25% total assets.
CNA Income Shares, Inc.	Diversified; 75% high-grade debt securities, 25% other debt securities, some with equity features. Approximate turnover rate 25%.
Current Income Shares, Inc.	Diversified; 75% high-grade debt securities, 25% other debt securities, some with equity features, and high-yield stocks. Approximate turnover rate 50%.
Drexel Bond Debenture Trading Fund	Diversified; 75% high-grade debt securities, 25% other bonds some with equity features. Approximately 190% turnover rate.
Excelsior Income Shares, Inc.	Diversified; 75% high-grade debt securities, 25% other bonds, some with equity features, no more than 20% private placements. Approximate turnover rate 10%.

Federated Income and Private Placement	Nondiversified; 80% in private-placement debt securities, many with equity features, 20% other debt securities.
Fort Dearborn Income Securities, Inc.	Diversified; 75% high-grade debt securities, 25% other bonds, some with equity features. Approximate turnover rate 35%.
Hattaras Income Securities, Inc.	Diversified; 70% in high-grade debt securities, 30% other bonds, some with equity features, preferred stock, and foreign debt securities. Currently holds approximately 15% short-term securities. Approximate turnover rate 90%
INA Investment Securities, Inc.	Diversified; 90% high-grade debt securities, 10% other bonds and preferred stock. Up to 50% securities with equity features and up to 25% private placements. Approximate turnover rate 95%.
Independence Square Income Securities, Inc.	Diversified; 60% high-grade debt securities, 40% other bonds and preferred stocks, up to 25% private placements.
Intercapital Income Securities, Inc.	Diversified; 75% either high-grade debt securities (at least 50%) or other high-grade securities with equity features, 25% other fixed-income securities. Approximate turnover rate 45%.
John Hancock Investors, Inc.	Diversified; 30% high-grade debt securities, up to 50% private placements, both preferred stock and common stock cannot exceed 20% (no more than 5% to a single issuer, and no more than 25% in one industry). Turnover rate not expected to exceed 30%.
John Hancock Income Securities, Inc.	Diversified; 75% high-grade debt securities, leverage up to 20% of total assets. Approximate turnover rate 9%.

TABLE 14

Closed-End Bond Funds' Investment Policies continued

Fund	Investment policy
Mass. Mutual Income Investors, Inc.	Diversified; 75% high-grade debt securities, 25% other bonds, some with equity features, preferred and common stock. Approximate turnover rate 45%.
Montgomery Street Income Securities	Diversified; 70% high-grade debt securities, 30% other bonds, some with equity features and preferred stocks. Maximum industry exposure 25%, and no individual issuers more than 5%.
Mutual of Omaha Interest Shares, Inc.	Diversified; 80% high-grade debt securities, 20% other bonds, and up to 10% private placements.
Pacific American Income Shares, Inc.	Diversified; 75% high-grade debt securities, 25% other fixed-income securities, some with equity features and preferred stocks, not more than 25% private placements, and leverage no more than 20%. Approximate turnover rate 30%.
St. Paul Securities Income, Inc.	Diversified; 75% high-grade debt securities, 25% other bonds, some with equity features and preferred stocks, up to 25% private placements, leverage not to exceed 20%. Approximate turnover rate 200%.
State Mutual Securities, Inc.	Nondiversified; at least 40% high-grade debt securities, up to 50% private placements, some with equity features, up to 10% other bonds, preferred and common stock, and leverage upt to 25%. Approximate turnover rate 15%.

Transamerica Income Shares, Inc.	Diversified; 80% fixed-income debt securities, up to 20% other securities with equity features. Approximate turnover rate 200%.
U.S. Life Income Funds, Inc.	Diversified; 50% high-grade debt securities, 50% other securities, up to 10% common shares, and up to 30% private placements, leverage up to 25% of total assets. Approximate turnover rate 120%.
Vestaur Securities, Inc.	Diversified; 75% high-grade debt securities, 25% other bonds, some with equity features, leverage up to 20% of total assets. Approximate turnover rate 75%.

Common Stocks:
The Best Inflation Hedge
for the 1980s

Between 1968 and 1979, the annual rate of return on common
stocks was a paltry 3.1 percent. During the 1980s, I believe that
figure will be around 15 percent—perhaps even more. Hard to
believe? Read on and you will find why common stocks have
reached their current sorry state and why their future is much
brighter (and yours too) if you invest now.

Where Has All the Money Gone?

Back in the 1960s, it was widely believed that sensible investors
should buy common stocks for generous long-run returns and for
protection against inflation. As was shown in Chapter 2, over the
long pull common stocks have produced an annual rate of return
of about 9 percent—considerably above the long-run rate of
inflation. Moreover, it seemed reasonable to suppose that equities, representing ownership claims on real property, would pro-

vide investors with long-run protection against inflation. After all, in an era of inflation, factories, equipment, and inventories should rise in value along with all other prices.

Let's face it, however, during the 1970s stock market investing has created a nouveau poor in the United States. The Dow Jones Industrial Average, which supposedly crossed the 1000 barrier "for good" in 1973, ended the decade of the 1970s still languishing near the 800 level. Because this disastrous performance occurred at the same time the general price level increased about 70 percent, it has now become fashionable to believe that stocks are no longer an effective hedge against inflation (if they ever were). Indeed, many financial writers claim that inflation destroys real earnings power and "swindles the equity investor." In 1979, *Business Week* published a cover story on the death of equities. Institutional investors who do not believe in capital punishment have understandably rushed to the sidelines and individuals have been consistent net sellers of their equity mutual funds. At the present time, few people are thanking Paine Webber, and even when E. F. Hutton talks, nobody listens.

Investors have recently found little comfort in the satisfactory long-run performance record of common stocks. They are all too well aware of Lord Keynes's admonition "In the long run we are all dead," and over the shorter run investors expect to enjoy themselves and earn satisfactory returns. The market has killed off most of its supporters during the last decade. A lot of money that fled the stock market wound up in gold and various objets d'art, investments whose prices have recently been far outdistancing inflation.

An interesting study was done in 1979 by Robert S. Salomon, Jr., of the renowned investment firm of Salomon Brothers. Salomon plotted the 1968–79 investment records of several major assets. The results in Table 15 leave little doubt as to the reason money has been leaving the stock market.

In the eleven years to 1979, common stocks actually underperformed long-term bonds, while gold, Chinese ceramics, stamps, and other nontraditional investments produced extraordinary returns. One is reminded of the story of the small boy on his first

TABLE 15
Traditional vs. Nontraditional Investments, 1968–1979

Investment	Compound annual growth in value, 1968–79
Gold	19.4%
Chinese ceramics	19.1
Stamps	18.9
Rare books	15.7
Silver	13.7
Coins (U.S. nongold)	12.7
Old master paintings	12.5
Diamonds	11.8
Farmland	11.3
Single-family house	9.6
U.S. consumer price index	6.5
Foreign currencies[a]	6.4
High-grade corporate bonds	5.8
Common stocks	3.1

SOURCE: Salomon Brothers
[a]West German mark, Japanese yen, Swiss franc, and Dutch guilder.

trip to an art museum who was told that a famous abstract paint-
ing was supposed to be a horse. "Well then," the boy wisely
asked, "if it's supposed to be a horse, why isn't it?" If common
stocks are supposed to be an inflation hedge, investors may legiti-
mately ask, why aren't they?

Why Has All the Money Gone?

The dissatisfaction with equities goes deeper, however, than
impatience with their performance during any particular period.
Many investors now feel that common stocks can no longer protect against inflation. These Wall Street nay-sayers believe that
recent inflation has caused corporate profits and dividend-paying

ability to shrink drastically, especially when appropriate inflation adjustments are made to the reported figures. Inflation is portrayed as a kind of financial neutron bomb; it leaves the structure of corporate enterprise intact but destroys the life blood of profits. In effect, this is a belief that our system has undergone a fundamental change, one in which profits will never return to former levels but rather will continue to decline without interruption. Since profits are the source of dividends and since increased earnings provide the underpinning for capital gains, these doomsayers see nothing but trouble for the stock market. The engine of capitalism seems to many investors to be running in reverse, and in such a case a walk down Wall Street—random or otherwise —might be quite unhealthy.

The specific thesis of those who take a more or less apocalyptic view of the world is that profits as a percentage of invested capital have shrunk considerably, especially over the late 1960s and early 1970s. Some seers see this profit squeeze continuing nonstop until, as Lord Keynes once put it, "the euthanasia" of the capitalist class results. Money has left the stock market for dividendless gold and breakable china because of this alleged profits squeeze, which is at the bottom of most of the badmouthing of common stocks.

But is the world such a depressing place these days? Are corporate profits—those record levels that were being reported by many companies in 1979—an illusion? Has inflation made emperor's clothes out of profits and the stock market as well? Let's round up the suspects, chief among them the alleged profits squeeze, and see who or what caused the market's decline.

Is It True What They Are Saying About Profits?

It used to be that profits were considered a relatively simple matter. They were the excess of income over expenses. Charles Dickens thought of profits as happiness and described them as such in *David Copperfield:* "Annual income twenty pounds, annual expenditure nineteen nineteen six, result happiness; annual in-

come twenty pounds, annual expenditure twenty pounds ought
and six, result misery."

In an era of inflation, figuring out true profitability can be quite
complex. The problem is that inflation tends to make reported
profits appear misleadingly large. Inflation swells reported
profits (as well as actual tax liabilities) through two fictitious
elements—the overstatement of income (because of the inclusion
of inventory profits) and the understatement of expenses (because depreciation charges are calculated on original rather than
replacement cost). Thus, we must be careful in looking at profits
to judge them as nearly as possible on a true economic basis and
to refrain from being misled by apparently satisfactory reported
earnings.

Inventory profits provide the same kind of illusory benefits for
a business firm that real estate gains provide for homeowners.
Homeowners have paper capital gains from the rising values of
their homes but, unless they obtain additional mortgages at high
interest rates, they cannot use this wealth as long as they live in
them. Even worse, as soon as their property is reassessed, property taxes go up. Similarly, inventory profits are not the benefit
to a firm that they seem. As the firm disposes of its appreciated
inventory, the goods must be replaced at higher prices. Thus,
inventory profits provide no cash flow for the firm. Indeed, just
the opposite is true, for these paper profits are taxed at regular
income tax rates.

Depreciation charges are another factor in the inflation-swol-
len profit picture. These are the expenses, charged against taxable income, for the wearing out of the firm's plant and equipment during the production process. The less the charge, the
more income (and profit) will be reported. Because depreciation
charges are based on low original rather than higher current
replacement cost, they are usually not as high as they should be.
This makes the remaining income appear as healthy profit when
it should be set aside to provide for the necessary replacement
of the depreciating assets.

These two factors—the overstatement of income because of

the inclusion of inventory profits, and the understatement of depreciation charges because of their calculation on the basis of original rather than replacement cost—have swelled reported taxable profits. They are, as I have just shown, fictitious elements in the profit picture and form the basis of the argument that profits ain't what they used to be.

But, as we all know, "there are lies, damned lies, and statistics." Most people forget that there is a further necessary inflation adjustment to reported profits: inflation reduces the real value of the firm's debt. Current accounting conventions ignore this fact. It is well known that bondholders suffer from inflation because they get paid back in dollars that have less purchasing power than the dollars originally invested. But the counterpart of the bond investors' loss is the bond issuer's gain. This gain never shows up in any of our profit figures—even the ones supposedly adjusted to account for inflation.

"Aha," you say, "but the bondholder realizes that he or she will lose in real purchasing power and for that reason demands an inflation premium in interest rates." True enough. Investors might happily buy long-term bonds at a 3-percent interest rate if no inflation were expected, but would demand and receive an 11-percent interest rate if inflation were expected to proceed at, say, 8 percent per year. The extra 8-percent interest can be considered an inflation premium that compensates the bondholder for the expected loss in real purchasing power of the original investment. For every $100 loaned to the corporation, the bondholder knows that $8 in real purchasing power will be lost after a year in which the inflation rate is 8 percent.

Thus, after bondholders realize that inflation will continue, interest rates will rise to provide adequate compensation for the expected inflation. But this is precisely the point. Our accounting conventions do penalize earnings for the inflation premiums contained in interest rates since *all* interest is deducted before calculating corporate profits. But the corresponding gain to the corporation that comes from the ability of the corporation to repay its debt in cheapened dollars is never considered. We ignore the fact that the $8 the bondholder loses in real purchasing power represents an $8 gain to the corporate borrower, who repays in dollars that are worth 8 percent less at the end of the year. And this gain to the corporation and its stockholders from the declining real value of corporate debt must be included in any valid measure of inflation-adjusted profits.

Figure 5 presents the development of fully adjusted corporate profits in the U.S. over the past quarter century. The numbers show clearly that there is no evidence that corporate profitability is in a long-run decline. While profits in the 1970s were certainly lower than they were in the mid-1960s, they were not much different in the late 1960s and 1970s from what they were in the late 1950s and early 1960s. What appears to be more of an

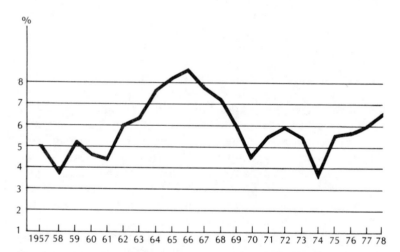

Figure 5. *Inflation-Adjusted Profits Related to Replacement Value of Equity Capital. The after-tax profits of nonfinancial corporations are adjusted to exclude inventory profits and to put depreciation on a replacement-cost basis. As inflation reduces the real value of corporation debt, this reduction is added back to profits. These adjusted profits are then divided by the nonfinancial corporate capital owned by equity holders (and valued at replacement cost).*

aberration is the period from the mid- to late 1960s when profit rates were unusually high and when the economy was characterized by "overfull" employment and flat-out capacity operations during our massive involvement in the Vietnam War. Even if profits fell somewhat during a recession in the early 1980s, the case would still hold. There is simply no evidence that true profits have been "sliding down a pole greased by cruel and inexorable inflation," as is widely believed in the financial community.

Has Dividend Growth Been Inadequate?

Perhaps, however, we are looking in the wrong place for a clue to the market's decline. Remember the well-known story of the government bureaucrat searching on his hands and knees on Pennsylvania Avenue for some object during the midday rush. "What are you looking for?" asked a passerby.
"My watch."
"Do you remember where you lost it?"
"Over on Connecticut Avenue."
"Then why are you looking here?"
"The light is better here."
There is much light placed on corporate earnings in the financial press; but perhaps the experts would be wiser to focus on dividends rather than earnings. Maybe the relevant question is not what earnings show—however adjusted—but rather what dividends U.S. corporations are able to pay. The acid test of whether true earning power is increasing is the ability of corporations to provide a stream of dividends whose growth will keep up with inflation. Let us then move our light over from earnings to dividends.
Figure 6 shows the progression of dividends over the past two decades as well as the inexorable upward march of the price level as measured by the Consumers Price Index. It is clear from the chart that dividends from the major U.S. corporations (as measured by the Standard & Poor's Composite Index) have outpaced

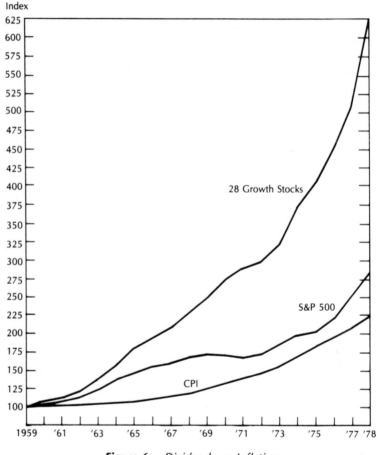

Figure 6.   *Dividends vs. Inflation*

inflation. Even more exciting is an index of the dividends of twenty-eight growth companies compiled by David L. Babson & Co; it far outdistances the CPI.[1] Clearly the problem does not lie in inadequate dividend growth.

[1]The names of the stocks in the Babson twenty-eight-stock growth index are listed in the Appendix to this chapter.

Are There Other Culprits Around?

Are we still looking in the wrong place? Could there be other fundamental changes in our economic system that spell the end of common stocks as sensible investments? Has our welfare state reduced the willingness of individuals to work? Government benefit payments to individuals rose rapidly in the 1970s, and undoubtedly their effect has been to induce some individuals to withdraw from work. Yet consider that the proportion and number of individuals working in the U.S. economy reached new highs in 1979.

Have high taxes drained the incentive of individuals to work and invest? Inflation puts us all in higher tax brackets and thus does tend to increase effective tax burdens on the real incomes of both corporations and individuals. But some gains are not taxed (such as the equity owners' gain at the expense of the bondholder), many taxes have been reduced (including corporate income and capital-gains taxes) and special breaks for investors (such as the liberalized Keogh plan discussed in the last chapter) have been adopted.

Are we now governed by what many people consider an immoral, incompetent, and socialist-leaning group of politicians? The 1970s did witness scandals in the highest office of the land and an energy crisis exacerbated by government policies. But politicians have probably changed little over the years, immorality has been with us since the Garden of Eden, and one suspects that the mood of our country at the start of the 1980s is probably more conservative than it has been for many years. High taxes and loss of faith in government have led to "Proposition 13" revolts, not to abdication.

Movie buffs will recall the marvelous final scene from *Casablanca*. Humphrey Bogart stands over the body of a Gestapo colonel, a smoking gun in his hand. Claude Rains, the inspector general, turns his glance from Bogart to the smoking gun to the dead colonel and finally to his assistant, and says, "The Gestapo colonel has been shot. Round up the usual suspects." We too have rounded up the usual suspects, but we have yet to find out who shot the stock market nor have we discovered a rational motive for the crime.

Why Is the Market Feeling So Bad?

If it is not a precipitous and irreversible drop in profitability and dividend-paying ability that is responsible for the market's malaise, why is the market feeling so bad? The major reason for the decline in equity prices is that investors' evaluation of earnings—the multiple they are willing to pay for a dollar of earnings—has fallen roughly in half. But why have multiples collapsed?

Two explanations are possible. The first has recently been offered by Franco Modigliani, an internationally respected financial economist. In an article in the *Financial Analysts Journal*, written with Richard Cohn, it was argued that the market is simply making a mistake. Modigliani and Cohn state that the market is just not capitalizing earnings properly in an era of inflation and that multiples have fallen to irrationally low levels.

This explanation is, of course, quite plausible. We saw in Chapter 1 that markets often overreact and get carried away in frenzies of speculative buying and fits of selling panic. The market may now be irrationally pessimistic, as perhaps it was unreasonably optimistic in the 1960s. Nevertheless, I do not find this explanation entirely convincing. While I am not a dyed-in-the-wool random walker, and while I don't argue that market prices are always necessarily correct, I do have a healthy respect for the market's judgment. Between the economics profession and the stock market, I would still place my bet on the stock market every time.

In my judgment, the problem may not be that the market is making a mistake but rather that investors now *correctly* demand much higher prospective rates of return from common stocks to compensate them for the sharply increased risks they perceive.[2] Investors in the mid to late 1960s saw the economic environment

[2]Economists often put the proposition in terms of risk premiums—that is, the extra return you can expect from an investment over and above the return from perfectly predictable short-term investments. According to this view the risk

as a very stable one and faced the future with feelings of consummate confidence. From the middle 1970s to end of the decade investors had good reason to view the economy as far less stable, and they looked to the future with considerable uncertainty.

In the mid-1960s inflation was only beginning to rear its ugly head and consumer prices had been relatively stable for a number of years. We even thought in those days that we could manipulate the economy so that recessions could be "fine-tuned" away: depressions were considered a curious anachronism. In short, the world seemed very stable. In retrospect, it is clear that this confidence and the associated high multiples assigned to earnings were not justified. Today, in contrast, there is in our country an almost palpable mood of uncertainty and pessimism. Who would have believed ten years ago that we could go through a period when the unemployment rate would approach 9 pecent or that the inflation rate would be measured in double digits, let alone that both could occur simultaneously as they did in the mid-1970s. Today the inflation rate remains at unprecedented high levels more usually associated with a banana republic than with the U.S. economy. This instability in our economic system has generated a mood of anxiety and foreboding about the future of the economy and about our ability to cope with our current economic problems.

Hand in hand with greater economic uncertainty and instability is a wider dispersion of potential outcomes and more unstable prospects for corporate enterprises. Thus, corporations' earnings available for their equity securities (dare I say equity insecurities?) are now quite rationally considered more variable and less dependable. Indeed, as investor sentiment has shifted to a fuller recognition of the risks of equity ownership, there may well have been an excessive reaction. There has been a tendency

premiums in the 1960s were very small—perhaps one or two percentage points. Now the premium investors demand to induce them to hold equities may be four to six percentage points. For example, now short-term rates on assets with no risk of principal loss are 11–12 percent while equities offer returns in the 15- to 18-percent range as I shall argue below. Thus, risk premiums for holding equities are in the four- to six-percentage-point range.

for uncertainty to turn to extreme pessimism. Murphy's law of "what can go wrong will go wrong" has been replaced by O'Toole's commentary, "Murphy was an optimist." As a consequence, investors have become reluctant to hold equities unless their prospective returns are raised by an increased "risk premium" appropriate to the new higher level of risk associated with equity ownership. Ironically, this is accomplished through a decline in stock prices relative to earnings so as to provide larger future returns consistent with the new riskier environment. Precisely because equities are perceived to have become riskier, investors have marked down their prices so that stocks can provide in the future an appropriately higher expected rate of return as compared with less risky assets.

The sickness of the stock market appears to result from a very sharp increase in the risk perceptions of investors; this in turn has caused a devastating mark-down in the evaluation of earnings (the price investors are willing to pay for a dollar of earnings). In early 1973, investors paid over $18 for a dollar of earnings for the Standard & Poor's Composite Index. Today, a dollar of the same earnings commands less than $8 in the market, as shown in Figure 7. Multiples of fast-growing companies suffered an even sharper drop. In early 1973 the multiple for the David Babson index of growth stocks (whose dividend growth was shown in Figure 6) was close to 30. At the end of 1979, it had fallen to less than 10. *It was the decline in multiples that prevented stock prices from reflecting the real underlying progress most companies made in earnings and dividend growth.* To be sure, this increase in risk premiums is related to inflation, which has made all long-term investment decisions more uncertain. But the result of these increased risk premiums is that stocks now offer *larger* anticipated rates of return to attract investors. While the falling stock prices associated with increased risk premiums have reduced rates of return over the past several years (and have in fact caused substantial losses, depending on the investment period covered), such price declines tend to increase investment returns in the future. This leads to a somewhat paradoxical conclusion: because stocks have been such a poor investment over the past several years, they

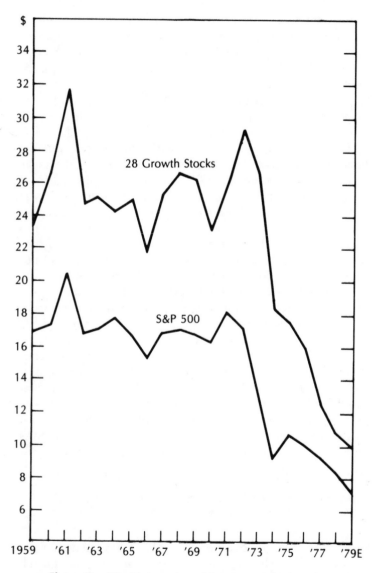

Figure 7. *The Contraction of Earnings Multiples: The Cost of $1 of Earnings*

should produce far more generous returns in the future.

The rather dismal recent history of common stocks is no reason to continue to avoid them. I am reminded of a conversation I overheard in a brokerage office a few years ago. A diligent account executive was vainly trying to sell a widow on a new issue of 11-percent bonds of extremely high quality. The widow's investment philosophy was a testimonial to Oscar Wilde's remark that experience is the name we give to our mistakes: "No," she said, "I have been buying bonds for the last decade and everyone of them has gone down. I'm experienced now and I will never be fool enough to buy bonds again." The widow was quite right that bonds had been a poor investment for many years. This was because investors had not anticipated the high rates of inflation the economy would suffer. Once investors realized that high rates of inflation were likely to persist, they lowered the prices they would pay for bonds until yields were sufficiently high so as to compensate bondholders for the new higher levels of inflation. Of course bonds had to fall, but this was necessary to make them a reasonably priced investment for the new economic environment. The situation is, of course, exactly the same for equities, which had to adjust both to the more generous bond yields associated with the higher inflation rates and to the much higher levels of perceived risk. But it is precisely the poor recent performance of equities that provides the price adjustments necessary to produce appropriately higher returns in the future. The issue is not how badly equity investors have done in the past several years—it is what might investors be kicking themselves about five years from now for not having bought today.

What Returns Are Likely from Stocks Purchased at Today's Prices?

We all know that the decade of the 1970s has been an absolutely dreadful one for equity investors. But now ask yourself what kinds of returns stock owners would have earned had they not suffered from the devastating fall in earnings multiples. Peter

"Let me put it this way. It's five years from now. What am I kicking myself for not having bought?"

Drawing by Whitney Darrow, Jr. © 1956 The New Yorker Magazine, Inc.

Bernstein, one of the most incisive and independent Wall Street analysts, has done just such a make-believe calculation. Bernstein starts his calculation in 1968 just as the market started to go to hell in a handbasket or in some other non-gas-powered vehicle. He asks, "Suppose that you could have bought common stocks in 1968 at today's price/earnings ratios: how would you have fared through the years of accelerating inflation, exploding interest rates, two major recessions, Penn Central, New York City,

Bank Herstatt, the virtual impeachment of a president, the Vietnam debacle, price and wage controls, and the demise of the dollar, just to name a few of the horrors that we have experienced during this dismal period?" Believe it or not, the answer is: Very well.

The Dow Jones Industrial Average earned $57.89 in 1968. If you bought the Average at the end of 1968 at eight times those earnings, you would have paid $463. You would have received $428 in dividends over the subsequent eleven years. At say, $850 —the actual average price for the Dow in 1979—your total return would have worked out to about 12 percent per annum through all the trauma of one of the most difficult decades in history. Dividends alone would have returned over 90 percent of the original investment, offsetting substantially all of the inflation over this period. Bernstein also points out, *"If you had been able to buy the Dow at 8X earnings in 1968 and held on [during the 1970s], the Average could be selling at [only] 5.5X earnings in 1979 and still would have provided you with a total return sufficient to have kept pace with inflation.* It would have had to sink to less than one times 1979's earnings to make your total return negative in nominal terms!"

Similar kinds of results can be obtained using the Standard & Poor's Index instead of the Dow. When the calculations are done with samples of growth companies, the results are even more favorable. The point is that were it not for the enormous drop in multiples, the returns from the market would have been excellent.

So, How Does All This Add up to 15 Percent?

We've just seen that had they purchased at today's P/E ratios, investors would have reaped 12 percent per year on stock purchases made in 1968. This substantial return is the result of growth performance of the dividends and earnings of common stocks over the decade. The fly in this sweet investment ointment was that the P/E ratio was at 18 in 1968 and it is the 10-point drop in this multiple that produced only mediocre results and soured people on the stock market. While Bernstein's analysis presents a very favorable picture of dividend performance, it doesn't tell us exactly what we can expect from here on out. I am convinced that at today's yields, dividends provide a financial base for even larger returns over the next decade.

Let's continue and see how you can obtain a 15-percent return, which will more than compensate for your fortitude in investing in stocks. I'm not going to promise you a rose garden, just a meat-and-potatoes stock like good old "Ma Bell" to justify my optimism and my assertion of a 15-percent return.

The American Telephone and Telegraph Company is not a spectacular investment but it is a high-quality bellwether stock and very widely held by the public. At the start of the 1980s the basic investing measurements for an AT&T share were as shown in Figure 8.

We see that, for openers, an investor can expect a 9.7-percent rate of return just from a continuation of the same $5 dividend. Ma Bell doesn't leap and bound, but she has been able to produce *growing* dividends. Even during the 1970s (a decade most equity investors would rather forget), the dividend grew at better than a 7½-percent rate. Let's be really cautious and suppose that during the 1980s the dividend grows at only a 5.8-percent rate (certainly a conservative assumption and actually somewhat below some estimates currently being made in Wall Street). Now we all know that when earnings and dividends grow at an average

Price: $51½
1980 Earnings (est.): $7.80
P/E Ratio: 6.6
1980 Dividend (est.): $5
Yield: 9.7%

Figure 8. *AT&T Early 1980 Investment Profile*

rate of, say, 5.8 percent, we don't expect the growth to come in
at exactly that rate in every year. Prosperous years for the economy may bring much larger increases—recession years could
even bring declines, especially in earnings. But let's suppose that
1981, for example, is an average year. We now have the picture
shown in Figure 9.

1981 Earnings (est.): $8.25 ($7.80 + 5.8%)
1981 Dividend (est.): $5.29 ($5.00 + 5.8%)

Figure 9.   *AT&T's 1981 Estimated Growth*

Before we can project an AT&T investor's overall rate of return during 1980—including both dividends and changes in the
worth of a share—we need to project what the stock price will be
at the start of 1981. Suppose we conservatively project that the
market will be just as pessimistic at the start of 1981 as it was at
the start of 1980. It's easier to get into a state of depression than
to get out of it (like the old saw about making love to a gorilla:
you don't quit when *you* get tired; you quit when the *gorilla* gets
tired). With the same degree of pessimism prevailing at the start
of 1981, the market would continue to assign a price/earnings
multiple of 6.6 and a dividend yield of 9.7 percent to AT&T
stock. Thus, it will sell at $54½ a share—6.6 times its earnings
of $8.25—while still producing a 9.7-percent yield on its then
projected $5.29 dividend (Figure 10). We have now completed
our investment profile.

Under these circumstances, the holder of AT&T stock can
expect a yearly return of 15½ percent—9.7 percent from the
dividend yield and 5.8 percent from the growth of the company
(Figure 11). The investor gets $5 in dividends and approximately

Price: $54½ (6.6 × $8.25 earnings)

1981 Earnings (est.): $8.25

P/E Ratio: 6.6

1981 Dividend (est.): $5.29

Yield: 9.7% ($5.29 dividend ÷ by $54½ price)

Figure 10. *AT&T's Early 1981 Estimated Investment Profile*

$3 in capital gains for a total return of $8—approximately 15½ percent of the original $51½ investment (because of rounding, the arithmetic comes out only approximately correct).

Purchase Price 1980: $51½

Market Price 1981: $54½

Capital Gain: $3

Dividend During

Period Held: $5

$$\frac{\text{Total Return}}{\text{Purchase Price}} = \frac{\$8}{\$51\frac{1}{2}} \approx 15\frac{1}{2}\%$$

Figure 11. *Returns to Holder of AT&T Stock (12 mos., early 1980 to early 1981)*

That seems almost too good to be true. And yet it's a conservative estimate. In general, the rule to use to find the prospective rate of return on any stock is to add the expected growth rate of the company to its dividend yield. The rule works whenever there is no change in the general level of P/E multiples or yields.

Just for fun, let's speculate a bit and change the rules of our game. Suppose that AT&T's P/E ratio goes up to 8, which is still far less than the 14 averaged during the 1960s and 1970s. As J. P. Morgan once remarked, "It always stops raining," and who knows—it could stop raining on the stock market too. With earnings of $8.25, a P/E of 8 would boost AT&T shares to $66. Look at the numbers in Figure 12. They could knock your socks off.

Purchase Price 1980: $51½

Market Price 1981: $66 (8 × $8.25)

Capital Gain: $14½

Dividend During
Period Held: $5

$$\frac{\text{Total Return}}{\text{Purchase Price}} = \frac{\$19\frac{1}{2}}{\$51\frac{1}{2}} \approx 38\%$$

Figure 12. *Possible Returns for Rose-Colored Glasses —Holders of AT&T Stock (12 mos., early 1980 to early 1981)*

The moral is clear. Even if the clouds don't lift, AT&T was priced at the start of the 1980s to provide quite a generous prospective return of 15½ percent. Indeed, the multiple could even fall a bit and the returns would still be acceptable. Any relief from the prevailing mood of uncertainty and pessimism, however, could bring spectacular returns—even to a staid "widow's and orphan's" stock like AT&T.

What about the rest of the market? It abounds with golden eggs. I've done similar calculations for the thirty stocks of the Dow Jones Industrial Average as of the start of the 1980s. When you add the dividend yields for each stock to the long-run growth rates, the prospective return is over 15 percent. (Growth rates are estimated by the Value Line Investment Service. Value Line regularly provides information on growth prospects for a wide variety of companies, and while these estimates are subject to considerable error, as I suggested in Chapter 2, the Value Line estimates have as good a record as anyone.) This average return of over 15 percent looks good either by historical equity standards or by the current yields available on long-term bonds.

I hope I've convinced you that there should be common stocks in your investment future. Their poor performance was due neither to deteriorating earnings nor to stagnant dividends; the real guilty party is the P/E ratio, which fell by more than half. Investor confidence plummeted from a feeling of certainty and overconfidence about the future in the mid-1960s to one of uncertainty and despair at this writing. But precisely because of that fall in multiples, common stocks are now priced to provide returns that are extremely generous, sufficient to offset even double-digit inflation and well above bond yeilds. Even if the present degree of uncertainty and foreboding continues, a balanced portfolio of common stocks should reward investors with an average return in excess of 15 percent per year.

Could I Be Wrong?

A popular maxim warns: "If you are calm when everyone around you is panicked, perhaps you don't understand the problem." Could the problem be worse than I have described? Might stocks continue to produce lackluster returns? Could the market actually be underestimating the long-run dangers to corporate profitability? No one can deny such a possibility. Paul Samuelson, when once discussing a brilliant academic colleague, described him as being "endowed with every gift except the gift of maybe." Even if there is no evidence that corporate profitability or dividend-paying ability has been damaged thus far, maybe they will suffer in the future.

One possible disaster scenario features *far greater* pressures by labor for real wage increases exceeding productivity growth, especially if labor feels pressed by increasing tax burdens. Such a struggle over the distribution of income could lead to a decline in the share of profits in national income. Another move to delight disaster enthusiasts would be unfavorable tax changes or an imposition of harsh price controls. These could so restrain profit growth that profits would no longer play their normal role of allocating investments to their most productive use. Presumably, the government would then play an increasing role in allocating profits directly to business firms (either unsuccessfully, as in the United Kingdom, or with some degree of effectiveness, as in Japan). This disaster scenario could also be embellished by recurring energy crises exacerbated by our growing dependence on foreign sources of petroleum.

The Stock Market, the Gnomes of Zurich, and the Edifice Complex

Unless we move to a wholly different overall economic system, however—and I see no evidence that we are traveling in that direction—it is unlikely that the role of the profit motive will be totally destroyed. I suspect that the economic, social, and political institutions of the U.S. are far more resilient and enduring than investors now believe. Fortunately, apocalyptic predictions seldom come true (and if they should, it is not clear what kind of property income would be safe). We dislike adversity and uncertainty, but we have a history of adjusting to and recovering from them. And remember, the market has already discounted a great deal of anticipated adversity.

Does this mean that I am predicting an immediate market rally from current price levels? Of course not. No one can predict short-term movements in the stock market, and perhaps we are better off for it. I am reminded of one of my favorite episodes from the marvelous old radio serial "I Love a Mystery." This mystery was about a greedy stock market investor who wished that just once he would be allowed to see the paper, with its stock price changes, twenty-four hours in advance. By some occult twist his wish was granted and early in the evening he received the late edition of the next evening's paper. He worked feverishly through the night planning his early morning purchases and late afternoon sales to guarantee him a killing in the market. Before his elation had diminished, he then read through the remainder of the paper where he found his own obituary. His servant found him dead the next morning.

Since I fortunately do not have access to future newspapers, I cannot tell how stock prices will behave in the weeks and months ahead. Indeed, as a random walker through Wall Street, I am skeptical that anyone can predict the course of short-term stock price movements. Nevertheless, my belief in the reasonable efficiency of markets leads me inevitably to the conclusion that, over the long pull, volatile common stocks are priced to yield more than staid fixed-income securities. And I do feel, to paraphrase the title of a 1960s book, that the stock market has been down so long it's beginning to look to me like up. Even old Ma Bell will provide plenty of profitable financial action. While there may be leaks in the house of capitalism, the roof does not appear to be caving in. The threats to equity investment now are probably not too different from other obstacles that common stocks have faced and overcome in the past.

I even think that a good "maybe" is that panic-depressive institutional investors have gone too far in discounting the risks to our economic system. Stock markets are either hot or cold, but seldom lukewarm. For the first time in decades, stocks are positively frigid and selling at prices below their book values—whether you compute these on historical costs or on current replacement costs of corporate assets. No wonder we read daily about takeover bids, where assets can be acquired at a small fraction of their real value. Moreover, at the start of the 1980s, the dividend yields on blue-chip stocks—such as the Dow Jones Industrial Average—was over 6 percent. This is the most favorable comparison with bonds that has existed in many years.

Given the recent speculation in such areas as office buildings and farmland, stocks today appear dirt cheap in an investment market where almost everything else is fully priced. Should the penumbra of uncertainty lift—as it might to the extent that the added risk premiums are due to overly pessimistic expectations with respect to profitability—stock investments could bring extraordinary returns. Even under current gloom-and-doom conditions, however, equities should still produce generous future returns. To be sure, a rapid *acceleration* of inflation would be likely to upset equity markets (through its effect in increasing risk perceptions rather than through any effects it has in reducing real profit rates). But unless you believe that *increasing* economic instability is inevitable, or that the profit system will face far different dangers in the future than it has in the past, I believe investors will be making a serious mistake if they now write off common stocks as unacceptable investments for a future period where the inflation rate is likely to remain high.

There is no doubt that we have severe problems. It seems that the only solution to our budget deficits is to merge with Saudi Arabia. The oil crisis provides real reason for concern as we pessimistically contemplate pouring booze into our gas tanks to drive our cars. Nuclear power is far from the risk-free panacea we had once hoped. But even mushroom clouds may have a silver lining. The wrenching adjustments that will be necessary for our economy during the 1980s provide enormous opportunities for profitable investment and for technological progress. Surely the country that invented the self-cleaning oven can find a way to develop alternative sources of energy. And the stock market appears to have discounted everything including a Martian invasion. The next investment folly may well be an excessive preoccupation with risk, which has literally paralyzed institutional portfolio managers and individual investors.

The best time to buy stocks is when no one wants them. All signs indicate that the start of the 1980s is such a time. Some bank trust departments are selling stocks to buy objets d'art for their customers. Individuals are warehousing commodities from gold to carpets—goods that gather dust, not dividends. Some institutions have developed an edifice complex—selling stocks at five to ten times earnings in order to buy buildings at twenty times earnings. In the late 1960s, individuals would hang on you like leaches at cocktail parties if they knew you "followed the market." In the late 1970s, you were left alone at the piano while they clung to real estate agents and talked about how much their houses were worth. The gnomes of Zurich, the international financiers who own billions of dollars, have only begun to nibble at the stock market. While I think no responsible advisor can predict when the next upturn in the market will occur, I am convinced that the analysis presented here leads inexorably to the conclusion that the major risk for investors today is the risk of being out of the stock market—not the risk of being in it.

Appendix

TABLE 16
Babson Growth Companies

Air Products and Chemicals, Inc.	Hewlett-Packard Co.
American Home Products Corp.	International Business Machines Corp.
AMP Incorporated	Johnson & Johnson
Burroughs Corporation	K Mart Corp.
Capital Holding Corp.	Marathon Oil Company
Citicorp	Merck and Company, Inc.
Coca-Cola Company	Minnesota Mining and Manufacturing Company
Colgate-Palmolive Co. (Delaware)	Pfizer Incorporated
Dow Chemical Co.	Proctor and Gamble Co.
Eastman Kodak Co.	Provident Life and Accident Insurance Company
Exxon Corporation	Revlon, Inc.
Georgia-Pacific Corporation	Sears, Roebuck and Company
Gillette Co.	Standard Brands Incorporated
Halliburton Co.	Xerox Corporation

CHAPTER 5

Beating the
Experts at Buying Stocks

It's time for specifics. How do you go about buying individual stocks? Basically, there are three ways: I call them the Easy Way, the Speculative System, and the Malkiel Method. In the first case you simply buy a share of the market index through a so-called index fund. You're assured of the market's rate of return—a return that I believe will average around 15 percent per year during the 1980s. This method also has the virtue of being absolutely simple. You send away one check, need make no further decisions, and you're guaranteed of earning the same yearly rate of return as the market, as measured by the Standard & Poor's 500 Stock Index. Under the second system, you pick your own stocks or investment managers and get *much higher* or *much lower* rates of return. This involves much more work than the easy way but, for those who wouldn't play the game any other way, much more fun. To help tilt the odds of success a bit more in your favor, I've given you a step-by-step guide for picking stocks. Finally, I present the Malkiel Method, which avoids stock picking yet promises that you will beat the experts at their own game. Even if the market is as highly efficient as suggested in Chapter 2, this strategy does offer a way of actually exceeding the market rate of return.

The Easy Way: Buying the Market

The Standard & Poor's 500 Stock Index, a composite that represents 70 percent of the value of all U.S. traded common stocks, beats most of the experts over the long pull. Thus, the easy way to pick stocks would be to buy a portfolio of all companies in this index. I argued back in 1973 (in the first edition of *A Random Walk Down Wall Street*) that the means to adopt this approach was sorely needed for the small investor:

What we need is a no-load, minimum-management-fee mutual fund that simply buys the hundreds of stocks making up the broad stock market averages and does no trading from security to security in an attempt to catch the winners. Whenever below-average performance on the part of any mutual fund is noticed, fund spokesmen are quick to point out, "You can't buy the averages." It's time the public could.

Shortly after my book was published, the "index fund" idea caught on. At first only large pension clients were offered this investment opportunity. But one of the great virtues of capitalism is that when there is a need for a product, someone usually finds the will to produce it. In 1976, a fund was created that allowed the public to get into the act as well. That fund, the First Index Investment Trust, is a mutual fund that is internally managed and therefore pays no investment advisory fee. The investments of the trust are the 500 stocks of the S&P 500 Stock Index, purchased in the same proportions as their weight in the index. Each investor shares proportionately in the net income and in the capital gains and losses of the fund's portfolio.

Since its inception, the First Index Investment Trust has closely "tracked" the S&P 500 Stock Index. There are no so-called loading fees for buying the trust's shares. Management expenses (custodian fees, collecting and distributing dividends, preparing summary reports for investors, etc.) run at less than 0.3 percent of assets, far less than the expenses incurred by most mutual funds or bank trust departments. You can now buy the market conveniently and inexpensively.[1] In fact, if you own any of the 500 stocks of the S&P, First Index allows you to trade it in, without brokerage expense, for shares of the Index Fund.

The logic behind this strategy is the logic of the efficient-market theory described in Chapter 2. The above-average performance of the S&P 500 Index compared with that of major institutional investors has been confirmed by Becker Securities Corporation, a firm specializing in compiling the track record of the experts managing corporate pension funds. For example, during the fifteen-year period ended on December 31, 1978, the S&P 500 outperformed 78 percent of the institutional investors in the Becker sample; the annualized total return for the S&P 500 was 1.1 percentage points better than the median fund in the Becker sample.

Similar data published in the *Pensions and Investments Performance Evaluation Report* analyze the investment returns of bank and insurance company pooled equity funds, revealing that the S&P 500 outperformed 93 of the 112 funds during the 1970s. Stock trading among institutional investors is like an isometric exercise: lots of energy is expended, but between one investment manager and another it all balances out, and both managers pay commissions that detract from performance. Like greyhounds at the dog track, professional money mangers seem destined to lose their race with the mechanical rabbit. Small wonder that many institutional investors, including Exxon, Ford, Western Electric, and New York Telephone, have put substantial amounts of their assets into index funds.

How about you? When you buy an index fund, you give up the

[1]A First Index prospectus and application form can be obtained by writing to P.O. Box 1100, Valley Forge, PA 19482, or by calling 800/523-7910. I must remind the reader that I am also a director of this fund.

chance of boasting around the golf club about the fantastic gains you've made in picking stock market winners. Broad diversification rules out extraordinary losses relative to the whole market; it also, by definition, rules out extraordinary gains. Thus, many Wall Street critics refer to index-fund investing as "guaranteed mediocrity." But experience conclusively shows that index-fund buyers are likely to exceed the results of the typical fund manager whose large advisory fees and substantial portfolio turnover tend to hamper investment results. And index investors will *predictably* receive the market return. Of course, this strategy does not rule out market risk: if the market goes down, your portfolio is guaranteed to follow suit. Many people will find the guarantee of playing the stock market game at par every round a very attractive one—especially with the market now priced to provide excellent returns in the 1980s.

The index method of investment has other attractions for the small investor. It enables investors to obtain very broad diversification with only a small investment. It also allows one to reduce brokerage charges. When an individual investor buys stocks, he or she pays a brokerage fee of about a dollar a share on small trades (even if a discount broker is used). The index fund, by pooling the moneys of many investors, trades in larger blocks and can negotiate a brokerage fee as low as five cents a share on its transactions. The index fund does all the work of collecting the dividends from the 500 stocks it owns and sending you one check a quarter (a check which, incidentally, can be reinvested in the fund if the investor desires). In short, the index fund is a sensible, serviceable method for obtaining the market's rate of return with absolutely no effort and at minimal expense.

I have only a few quibbles with the easy way of index investing. First, while the S&P 500 represents 70 percent of U.S. stocks, the 30 percent it excludes may be precisely the kind of emerging growth companies that offer higher rewards (as well as higher risks). It would be nice to have a fund available that bought an index of smaller companies—such as perhaps the companies in the American Stock Exchange index with its heavy weighting of younger growth companies and natural resource stocks. It would also be nice to have an international index fund. Second, the easy way, while sensible and useful, is a very dull way to enter the market. Those with speculative temperaments will undoubtedly prefer an alternative method of investing that involves at least trying to pick winners. Finally, the Malkiel Method described below, while somewhat harder to implement than index investing, will enable an investor to attain somewhat better performance than the index at no greater risk.

The Speculative System: Doing It Yourself

Picking Individual Common Stocks

Having been smitten with the gambling urge since birth, I can well understand why many investors have not only a compulsion to pick the big winners on their own but also a total lack of interest in a system that only promises results equivalent to the market as a whole. The problem is that it takes a lot of work to do it yourself and, as I've repeatedly shown, consistent winners are very rare. If you regard investing as play, however, this section demonstrates how a sensible strategy can produce substantial rewards and, at the very least, minimizes the risks in playing the stock-picking game.

Before putting my strategy to work, however, it's necessary to know the sources of investment information and how to choose an appropriate broker. Most information sources can be obtained at public libraries. You should be an avid reader of the financial pages of daily newspapers, particularly the *New York Times* and the *Wall Street Journal.* Weeklies such as *Barron's,* the *Commercial and Financial Chronicle,* and the *Wall Street Transcript,* should also be on your "must read" list. Business magazines such as *Business Week, Fortune,* and *Forbes* are also valuable in gaining exposure to investment ideas. The major investment advisory services are also good. You should, for example, try to have access to Standard & Poor's *Outlook* and the *Value Line Investment Service.* The first is a weekly publication which contains lists of recommendations and the second presents historical records, current reviews, and risk (beta) ratings of about 1550 securities as well as weekly recommendations.

With regard to a broker, it may not pay to utilize the discount firms recommended in Commandment IX if you really do want help. The most important criterion for an investor who wants to be exposed to investment ideas is to select a brokerage firm that can furnish investment information. The major question to ask is: Does your broker's firm have a large and well-respected research department? Does it produce comprehensive research reports—as opposed to one-page fly sheets—on the major investment alternatives? The firm should also be one that does a substantial amount of institutional business, ensuring your contact with the ideas that are making the rounds of the investment community. While, on average, the value of these reports and ideas may be nil, you've got to be exposed to them if you truly believe you are one of the rare individuals who can consistently win the game of guessing which idea is likely to catch on. Armed with solid information sources and a good broker, you can then begin the process of selecting individual stocks.

When writing *A Random Walk Down Wall Street* in the early 1970s, I proposed four rules for successful stock selection. In thinking about these rules for the 1980s, I find them just as serviceable today. Indeed, as I'll argue below, the present stock market environment is especially conducive to their success. In abridged form, the rules are as follows:

Rule 1. Confine stock purchases to companies that appear able to sustain above-average earnings growth for at least five years. As difficult as the job may be, picking stocks whose earnings grow is the name of the game. Consistent growth not only increases the earnings and dividends of the company, but may also increase the multiple that the market is willing to pay for those earnings. (This would further boost your gains.) Thus, the purchaser of a stock whose earnings begin to grow rapidly has a chance of a potential double benefit—both the earnings and the multiple may increase.

Rule 2. Never pay more for a stock than can reasonably be justified by a firm foundation of value. While I am convinced that you can never judge the exact intrinsic value of a stock, I do feel that you can roughly gauge when a stock seems to be reasonably priced. The market P/E is a good place to start: You should buy stocks selling at multiples in line with, or not very much above, this ratio. My strategy then is to look for growth situations that the market has not already recognized by bidding the stock's earnings multiple to a large premium. If the growth actually takes place you will often get a double bonus—both the earnings and the price/earnings multiple can rise, producing large gains. Beware of very-high-multiple stocks where many years of growth are already discounted in the price of the stock. If earnings decline rather than grow you will usually get double trouble—both the earnings and the multiple drop, causing heavy losses.[2]

Rule 3. It helps to buy stocks whose stories of anticipated growth are ones on which investors can build castles in the air. I stressed in Chapter 1 the importance of psychological elements in stock price determination. Individual and institutional investors are not computers that calculate warranted price/earnings multiples and print out buy and sell decisions. They are emotional human beings—driven by greed, gambling instinct, hope, and fear in their stock market decisions. This is why successful investing demands both intellectual and psychological acuteness. Of course, the market is not totally subjective either; if a growth rate appears to be established, the stock is almost certain to attract some type of following. But stocks are like people—what stimulates one may leave another cold, and the multiple improvement may be smaller and slower to be realized if the story never catches on. The key to success is being where other investors will

---

[2] I hate people who say "I told you so," but I make an exception for myself. In 1973, I cautioned readers not to buy those premier growth stocks (the one-decision Nifty Fifty stocks) whose multiples had soared in some cases to as much as sixty, seventy, and eighty times earnings and I mentioned several of those stocks by name. Following Rule 2, therefore, could have enabled you to avoid one of the most notorious investment follies of the 1970s.

be several months before they get there. So my advice is to ask yourself whether the story about your stock is one that is likely to catch the fancy of the crowd. Is it a story from which contagious dreams can be generated? Is it a story on which investors can build castles in the air—but castles in the air that really rest on a firm foundation?

Rule 4. Trade as little as possible. I agree with the Wall Street maxim "Ride the winners and sell the losers," but not because I believe in technical analysis. Frequent switching accomplishes nothing but subsidizing your broker and increasing your tax burden if you have realized gains. I do not say "Never sell a stock on which you have a gain." The circumstances that led you to buy the stock may change and, especially when it gets to be tulip time in the market, many of your successful growth stocks may get way overpriced as they did during the Nifty Fifty craze of the 1970s described in Chapter 2. But it is very difficult to recognize the proper time to sell, and there can be heavy tax costs involved. My own philosophy leads me to minimize trading as much as possible. I am merciless with the losers, however. With few exceptions, I sell out any stocks on which I have a loss before the end of each calendar year. The reason is that losses are deductible (up to certain amounts) for tax purposes, or can offset gains you may already have taken. Thus, taking losses can actually reduce the amount of loss. For example, if you are in the 50-percent tax bracket and have $1000 of short-term capital losses (the sale to give you a loss was made within a year of the purchase) and no other gains or losses, you can deduct the loss from your income and pay $500 less in taxes. I don't always take all losses. If the growth I expect begins to materialize and if I am convinced my stock will work out a bit later I might hold on a while. But I do not recommend too much patience in losing situations, especially when prompt action can produce immediate tax benefits.

Do these rules work? They have for me and they have for some of the few truly successful fund managers on the street. But perhaps it might be instructive to see how a couple I know put these rules into effect after reading the first edition of *A Random Walk Down Wall Street.*

This couple, whom I shall call the Smiths, took my advice about being avid readers of investment information seriously. In addition to the printed material I mentioned earlier, they already owned shares in two mutual funds and they used these as a source of information also. Every quarter when the funds reported their purchases, the Smiths would examine the stocks and see if they met my criteria. That was how they came across a company called Tyler. Smith Barney Equity Fund had bought a large block of shares in the first quarter of 1976. By the time the Smiths received the Smith Barney report, Tyler was selling at 17. It had a good growth record, was expected to continue to grow, and had a P/E slightly below the market average. While it was in a fairly prosaic heavy industrial business, it did seem to be attracting institutional interest, especially since Smith Barney, a firm with a highly respected research department, was recommending the stock. It seemed to satisfy my first three rules and so the Smiths bought some shares. Two years later, Tyler was selling at a robust 23 but it reported a decline in earnings for the first quarter. The Smiths did not know where to turn for advice about the stock. They did call their broker; he recommended a sale, and so they decided to "take their money and run." A month later, Tyler stock was selling at 32. The Smiths had made a nice profit on their investment, but it did hurt a bit to realize how much more they could have gained if they had followed my Rule 4. Their only consolation—of a sort—was when the Smith Barney Equity Fund report came out and they read that the "experts" had sold Tyler at precisely the same time they did.

The Smiths happen to like *Forbes* magazine as a source of investment advice; in the back of each week's issue, various columnists give specific recommendations and their reasons for such recommendations. In this way, they read about American Air Filter. The Smiths liked this company for its well-intentioned activities—it was in the business of ensuring clean air—and also more practical reasons: it had a good growth record and was in an area that would continue to grow because of governmental regulations. The P/E fell within my guidelines of being only three points above the market average. The Smiths also felt that increasing public interest in environmental control might spark the psychological interest of my Rule 3. They bought the company at 24, which turned out to be the high for the 1977 year. The company's stock price started to slide and then plunged below 20. The Smiths were not sleeping well over this purchase and considered selling it, according to my Rule 4. But, in fact, the financial figures for the company continued to be good and its future outlook remained promising. As it turned out, the market never did catch on to American Air Filter—but Allis Chalmers did, and one day the Smiths opened the *New York Times* to read that the company was being bought at $34 a share. The Smiths were lucky in this case, but following my Rules 1 and 2 helped also. Because there was a firm foundation of value, another company recognized the worth of American Air Filter even if the market had not.

Mrs. Smith is a writer and in preparing a spring newsletter for a research firm in Princeton she came across a U.S. Department of Agriculture report that consumption of chicken would increase dramatically by fall, primarily because beef prices would be staging a sharp upsurge. Shortly after digesting that piece of information, she was reading the dividend increases reported in *Barron's* and noticed that a company named Conagra had increased its dividend to yield 6 percent on the stock price. That seemed attractive, especially when she noticed that the P/E was 4, about half that of the market. She called her broker and got more information as well as a Standard & Poor's summary report. Conagra was a leading marketer of chicken. It had been through a great deal of financial troubles but had recently been reorganized; the company reported the dividend increase as a sign that it was interested in attracting stockholder support and that its financial health was back.

Now Conagra did not totally meet my Rule 1 criterion that it have extraordinary prospective long-run earnings growth. Mrs. Smith, however, knew, based on the USDA report, that over the next year or two it certainly would have good short-run growth.

Adding this to the extremely low multiple and the belief that rising food prices would lead other investors to search out those companies that would especially benefit from such inflation, Mrs. Smith felt that her overall rate of return would be favorable with a Conagra purchase. She bought the stock at 16 and in a little over a year it was up to 25. She felt rather pleased with herself when she read a "Heard on the Street" column in the *Wall Street Journal* that described the stock's dramatic recovery and mentioned that savvy investors bought the stock at 16. By late 1978, the stock's multiple was still below market level but Mrs. Smith felt that since she wasn't really sure about the firm's long-run prospects, it might be prudent to sell at a price in the low 20s, which she did.

The Smiths experiences illustrate the potential profits, pitfalls, and fun from employing my strategy. On the whole, the Smiths did very well and had a great deal of fun following my rules: their rate of return has far exceeded that recorded for the Dow Jones Industrials, the S&P 500, and the New York Stock Exchange Index. It took a lot of effort on their part, however. Generally, they spent five hours a week gathering and evaluating information on investment sources. There were also the nights when they did not sleep well; when, for example, their American Air Filter shares plunged by one-third of their purchase price. Since each purchase amounted to a large share of their total portfolio, the Smiths really took on a great deal of risk. The Smiths were undiversified—they had all their eggs in just two or three baskets. One really disastrous investment would have wiped out a substantial share of their capital. They also felt a keen sense of ignorance in that they were not always sure they could trust reported earnings, and they did not have the contacts and the up-to-the-minute information that the "experts" have access to. They realize that once a story is out in the regular press, it's unlikely that the market hasn't taken account of the information as the efficient-market theory supposes. They still feel that they are neophytes in a very tricky business and agree with me that picking individual stocks is like breeding thoroughbred porcupines. You study and study and make up your mind, and then proceed very carefully. In the final analysis, as much as I hope their excellent record resulted from following my good advice, their success may have mainly been the result of luck.

For all its hazards, picking individual stocks is a fascinating game. My rules do, I believe, tilt the odds in your favor while protecting you from the excessive risk involved in high-multiple stocks. I also believe that the present market environment could not be more favorable for the successful application of my rules. The reason is that like a closing accordian, the price/earnings multiples of stocks with superior growth prospects and those of the more prosaic stocks have come together. Because the last speculative investment craze involved the overpricing of the premier growth stocks, it is not unusual that the market has probably overreacted by probably underpricing these stocks now relative to the market. Figure 7, in the last chapter, showing the contraction of multiples for the S&P Index and for the Babson 28 Growth Stock Index has been redrawn as Figure 13 to show the contraction of *relative* multiples, specifically the multiple of the Babson 28 Growth Stock Index relative to that of the S&P 500. While growth stocks tended to sell at more than double the multiple of the S&P at the height of the "one-decision Nifty Fifty" craze in 1973, these stocks now sell at only a 10-percent premium to more run-of-the-mill stocks. Now, precisely the most interesting stocks in the market—those whose earnings and dividends have been far outdistancing inflation—are selling at their most reasonable market valuations in years. Thus, I believe that the start of the 1980s is the ideal time to pick individual stocks on the basis of my rules. Unlike the early 1970s, it will not be hard to find an abundant selection of strong companies that fill the bill.

But remember that a large number of other investors—including the pros—are trying to play the same game. And the efficient-market theory suggests that the odds of anyone's consistently beating the market are pretty slim. Nevertheless, for many of us, trying to outguess the market is a game that is much too much fun to give up. Even if you were convinced you would not do any

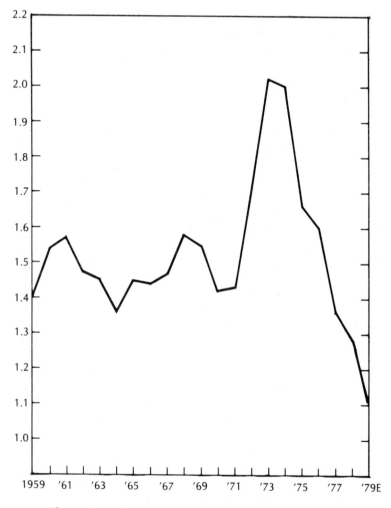

Figure 13. *The Premium for Growth Stocks (P/E of Babson Growth Stocks Relative to S&P Index)*

better than average, I'm sure that most of you with speculative temperaments would still want to keep on playing the game of selecting individual stocks.

Picking the Manager

There's an easier, more profitable way to gamble in the race for investment performance: instead of pricing the individual horses (stocks), pick the best jockeys (investment managers). These "jockeys" come in the form of mutual-fund managers, and there are over four-hundred for you to pick from.

In addition to offering risk reduction through diversification, these funds provide freedom from having to select stocks, and relief from paperwork and record keeping for tax purposes. Most funds also offer a variety of special services such as automatic reinvestment of dividends and regular cash-withdrawal plans. Mutual funds are particularly attractive as an investment vehicle for the establishment of Individual Retirement Accounts and Keogh plans described in Chapter 3.

While some readers may well be disappointed that I do not "name" stocks in this book, I have absolutely no hesitation about citing mutual fund managers who run their portfolios by following rules similar to the rules I use and who have enjoyed perfectly splendid records. John Marks Templeton is one such person.

You may recall that in Chapter 2, when I was demonstrating how unreliable and temporary superior performance really was, one exception stood out: the Templeton Growth Fund was not only in the top twenty during the go-go year of 1968, but it remained in the top twenty over the next ten years, racking up a total gain of over 300 percent.

According to every mutual fund rating service, the fund that bears John Marks Templeton's name has been the outstanding performer over the past two decades. Indeed, Templeton's record of beating the broad stock indexes extends as far back as the 1930s. In a field crowded with mediocrity, Templeton seems to be one of the true investment greats—a living embarrassment to the efficient-market theory.

This exception to the rule is a most unusual individual. A former Rhodes scholar, Templeton is a fervently religious man who believes in an omnipotent God who transcends narrow religious sects. Templeton starts each investment meeting with a prayer. He once told an interviewer, "We don't pray that our stocks will go up. We pray because it makes us think more clearly." He keeps a sense of detachment from the waves of euphoria and despair on Wall Street by running his portfolio from the quiet seclusion of Lyford Cay in the Bahamas.

Templeton's basic technique is to search out low-multiple stocks that rest on the firmest foundation of value, and then to have patience while the market catches up to him. If the anticipated earnings growth materializes, he expects to be rewarded with substantial capital appreciation both from the earnings growth and from an increase in the earnings multiple. Templeton's religious ecumenism extends to the stock market as well. Templeton seeks out the best bargains wherever they are to be found—however well known the company and whatever country in which it is located. For example, following World War II, he invested heavily in Europe because its stocks were cheap and because he felt European business would grow rapidly with the help of the Marshall Plan. Since then he has moved in and out of the Canadian and Japanese markets. It matters not whether the companies are in Seoul or Sandusky, Melbourne or Mexico City. Templeton's concern is that he owns stocks whose selling prices are lowest in relationship to their "true worth."

Right now, Templeton believes that the U.S. market represents the best bargain in the world. He feels U.S. stocks are now a better hedge against inflation than antiques, gold, or diamonds. He said, "Real estate is priced at twice what it was ten years ago, whereas common stocks are cheaper than they were then." He believes that eventually investors will be attracted to U.S. common stocks to keep ahead of inflation just as they recently have been running to gold and real estate. You can see why Templeton's style of management appeals to me.

One reasonable investment strategy is to bet that Templeton's outstanding record will continue. I only have two quibbles with this strategy: first, Templeton's fund is a load fund. A small investor has to pay an 8½ percent service charge just to buy in. It will therefore take a considerable period of above-average performance just to get back to even. Second, Templeton is now sixty-seven years old. While I am perfectly willing to believe that God is in fact on his side and will remain so, even Moses didn't live forever.

A younger version of John Templeton is the brilliant forty-eight-year-old portfolio manager for the Windsor Fund, John Neff. The Windsor track record under Neff is not as long as Templeton's, but during recent periods it was almost as fast. During 1975 and 1976, Windsor outperformed every fund in the nation with assets over $100 million. His record over longer periods is also exceptional. Like Templeton, Neff is an inveterate bargain hunter. His motto: "Get 'em while they're cold." His philosophy: "At Windsor we court the down-trodden and misunderstood and overlooked." His nickname: "The Contrarian."

Neff is particularly fond of what he calls "lesser recognized" or "secondary growth stocks"—stocks with growth characteristics but with nongrowth multiples. Neff uses a handy rule of thumb for stock selection: "I take current yield plus the earnings growth rate [this is what I called "prospective return" in Chapter 4] and divide it by the current price/earnings ratio. This means I am dividing what I am getting by what I am paying. If the answer is two or more, it's a buy."

It used to be hard to find stocks that met the test. Now under Neff's system even venerable AT&T is a buy. Recall that the prospective return (dividend yield plus growth) was about 15½ percent while the earnings multiple was under 7. Today, Neff is able to include many stocks in his portfolio where the prospective return is over three times the earnings multiple. The current market is made for the Neff system. If stocks are in the doghouse, Neff says, "Fine—then it's time to buy dogs." "I'm not smart enough to call the bottom," said Neff recently, "but I don't need to be with all the outstanding bargains around."

So Neff's system is to look for good value in terms of prospective return, which is priced at a low multiple. Then he patiently waits for Wall Street (or would-be acquirers) to pick up the scent. The key to success is, in his own words, "Have guts and be right." John Neff certainly has guts and thus far he has usually been right.

Has Neff ever been wrong? Yes, in 1972 Neff was dead wrong on the market and found himself in the bottom half of the performance derby. But it is that performance in 1972 that makes me especially fond of Neff as a portfolio manager. For 1972 was the year of the rush to the one-decision stock (as described in Chapter 1) and the only stocks that were doing well were those recognized growth stocks with multiples rising to 50, 60, 70, or more. Neff was quoted in *Forbes* in early 1973 as follows:

"My problem," Neff says, "is that up to last July almost all the market advance has come from growth stocks with silly multiples, stocks that I won't touch at these prices.

"Okay, you may say, 'You dummy, you, why aren't you there where the action is?' and I say, 'The hell with it. I won't take the risk.' "

It's a contrarian philosophy like this that lets Windsor Fund shareholders sleep well at night while still enjoying excellent long-run performance.

Table 17 (p. 166) presents data on five mutual funds, each with an outstanding long-term record—a feat particularly noteworthy in view of the difficult recent market environment. The clear lesson of Chapter 2 is that you can't count on these outstanding results persisting. But unlike the majority of the top performing funds of 1968, these funds have not achieved their records by being on the bandwagon of a popular fad. They do not take on excessive risk—indeed, their volatility (beta) ratings are (except in one instance) just about the same as for the Standard & Poor's Index. All these funds have a philosophy of hunting for value. While you have no guarantee that these portfolio managers will continue to beat the market, at least you know they did not achieve their records by building castles in the air. Being a gambling man, even a mostly random walker like me would rather place my bets on these funds than on the market as a whole.

The Malkiel Method: Buying at a Discount

Most of us are curious to know who our doctor uses when he is ill, or who the dentist goes to when his teeth are hurting. In a similar vein, many of you may wonder what stocks I buy. I don't get them wholesale, but I do buy at a discount. The discount is one of the little-known facts of the market.

Your broker could, if he or she wanted to, run an advertisement, such as the following, in the newspaper and actually deliver on the promise:

COMMON STOCKS AT A DISCOUNT

Gilt-edge securities, in mint condition, now selling at 25% discounts. Shares available in all the blue chips, including IBM, AT&T, Exxon, and many more. Securities available in diversified portfolios selling at 75¢ on the dollar.

You can buy portfolios of blue-chip securities at substantial discounts at the present time through a special type of mutual fund called a closed-end investment company.

Regular Closed-End Funds

There are two broad categories of mutual funds: open end and closed end. Open-end mutual funds—the kinds mentioned in the preceding section—issue and redeem shares at the net asset value of the share at the time of the transaction. They are "open" because the number of shares in the fund can increase indefinitely. Closed-end funds (officially called closed-end investment companies), on the other hand, neither issue nor redeem shares after the original offering. Thereafter, if an investor wants to sell or buy closed-end fund shares, he must do so on the market— generally on the New York Stock Exchange. The price of the shares depends on what other investors are willing to pay for them and is not necessarily related to net asset value, as is true of the open-end funds. Thus, closed-end funds can sell at a premium above or at a discount below their net asset values. In

TABLE 17

Selected Mutual Funds with Good Performance Records

Fund	Sales charge (%)	Year organized	Minimum amount initial purchase ($)	Minimum amount subsequent purchases	Expense ratio (%, 1978)	Total net assets (in $ millions, 6/30/79)	% change in net assets per share with capital gains accepted in shares and income dividends reinvested (to 6/30/79)		Rate of portfolio turnover (% of average assets) 1979	% Yield last 12 months (6/30/79)	Risk level (beta coefficient, three years to 11/30/79)	Payroll deduction or bank draft payment plan available	Keogh plan available	Individual retirement plan available
							5½ years	10½ years						
Fidelity Equity Income Fund 82 Devonshire Street Boston, MA 02109 800/225-6190	none	1965	500	50	1.00	77.9	138.7	75.5	101	5.4	1.00	X	X	X
Mutual Shares Corporation 170 Broadway New York, NY 10038 212/267-4200	none	1949	1000	none	0.95	66.8	277.7	214.6	49	2.3	0.83	—	X	X

Templeton Growth Fund 155 University Avenue Toronto M5H 3B7, Canada 800/237-0738	8.5[b]	1954	500	25	0.70	265.2	195.8	514.4	23	1.2	1.02	X	X	—
20th Century Investors Growth Fund 605 West 47th Street Kansas City, MO 64112 816/531-5575	none	1957	no min.	none	1.73	35.1	225.1	126.4	137	0.0	2.02	X	X	X
Windsor Fund[a] P.O. Box 1100 Valley Forge, PA 19482 800/523-7910 (800/362-7688 in Pa.)	none	1958	500	50	0.67	701.5	143.5	121.9	31	4.4	1.10	X	X	X

[a] I am a director of this fund.
[b] Actually ranging from 8.5% to .5%, depending on amount of purchase.

fact, these funds have been selling at substantial discounts from their net asset values. Closed-end funds hire professional managers, but their expenses are no higher than ordinary mutual funds. So even if you believe in professional investment management, here is a way to buy it at a discount. One of the closed-end funds I'll mention below is run by John Neff.

Why should such discounts exist? Many reasons have been offered, but none of them holds up on careful analysis. It's been suggested that some of the closed-end companies have been too conservatively managed and have invested in lackluster stocks with relatively low average returns. This has been true of some of the companies in the past. Many have had mediocre past records, but others have done quite well, and now the portfolios of most of the closed-end companies are little different from their open-end cousins.

Others have argued that the discounts can be explained by the existence of unrealized capital gains in the funds' portfolios that could affect the timing of an individual's tax liabilities. It is true that funds with larger amounts of unrealized appreciation do tend to sell at bigger discounts. But the tax effect is very small, and funds with no unrealized appreciation at all sell at large discounts.

Another explanation of the discount on some funds has to do with their practice of buying "letter" stock, the sale of which is restricted. Since the shares are generally highly illiquid, the market prices of these stocks are not a fair indication of their value on liquidation. Funds with large amounts of letter stock do, therefore, sell at relatively large discounts from their asset values. Nevertheless, the funds I have listed in Table 18 have only moderate amounts of (and in many cases, no) restricted stock, and this factor cannot explain the large discounts on these companies.

A final explanation for the discounts is offered by some efficient-market theorists who argue that the discounts reflect the negative value of the expenses of the funds including those paid for the "worthless" investment advisors. But remember, even running an index fund involves some cost and the additional expenses charged by the closed-end companies could at best explain only a small fraction of the market discount.

My own explanation for the existence of discounts on well-diversified investment companies is that they are not supported by an active marketing campaign. Once the fund has been established and closed, the investment advisor who typically organizes and brings out the fund does not stand to gain or lose in terms of the fees he earns. Thus, the advisor has no financial interest in promoting such funds on a continuing basis, unless he fears that a large discount will engender a takeover bid that leaves the manager out of a job. Moreover, brokers, through whom shares must be purchased, may well prefer to sell load-type open-end funds on which the broker will earn a larger commision. The truth of the matter is that, to the dismay of economists, investment funds are not *bought;* rather, they are *sold* by brokers, other salesman, or, in the case of no-load funds, by a combination of advertising and direct solicitation. Since virtually no "sales" effort is made on behalf of closed-end funds—because there is no possible payoff to such an effort in terms of increasing the fund's assets—the discounts may reflect scarcity of buyers relative to sellers.

A second and related possibility is that the discount on such funds is to some extent the functional equivalent of the redemption feature of open-end funds. Most open-end equity funds in recent years have suffered from redemptions in excess of new sales, reflecting the public's aversion to common stocks and their preference for the more stable money-market vehicles. Since shares cannot be redeemed in a closed-end fund, the discounts may reflect the present state of the public's aversion to equities.

In any case, rational economic arguments can explain only a small part of the discounts that have typically existed. I think that some of the discount represents a market inefficiency. As a result, closed-end funds are a great way to buy the "market at a discount."

Once again, I'm willing to back my words with names. The funds in Table 18 at the indicated discounts represent unusually good value.

Suppose, however, that the discounts as of June 1979 are not

TABLE 18
Selected Closed-End Funds

Fund	Price (6/30/79)[a]	Discount (6/30/79)[a]	Average discount past 15 years	Risk level (beta)
Baker Fentress	42½ bid	40.6%	not available for 15 years	1.19
Lehman	10⅝	27.6	7	1.18
General American Investors	10⅞	28.1	10	.95
Madison	14½	26.4	3	1.01
Niagara Shares	11	28.3	6	.84
Tri Continental Corp.	17½	25.1	16	1.12
U.S. & Foreign Securities	16½	27.9	19	.92
Adams Express	11¼	24.1	11	.55

[a]SOURCE: *Wall Street Journal* for current prices and discounts. Past discounts are calculated from Wiesenberger Investment Services. Betas are from Computer Directions Advisers, Inc.

a historical abberation but rather a sign of things to come. Suppose that the high discounts are here to stay. What good does it do you? Think about it for a moment. For every dollar you put into the fund, you will have more than a dollar invested on which dividends can be earned. So even if the fund just equals the market return, as believers in random walk would expect, you will beat the averages.

It's like having a $100 savings account paying 5-percent interest. You deposit $100 and earn $5 interest each year. Only this savings account can be bought at a 25-percent discount; in other words, for $75. You would still get $5 interest (5 percent of $100), but since you only paid $75 for the account, your rate of return is 6.67 percent (5 ÷ 75). Note that this increase in yield is not predicated on the discount's narrowing at all. Even if you get only $75 back when you cash in, you will still get a big bonus in extra return for as long as you hold the account. The discount on closed-end funds provides a similar bonus. You get your share of dividends from a full dollar of assets, even though you pay only seventy-five cents for it.

Some analysts believe that pressure from shareholders will force the investment advisers who control regular closed-end funds to convert them to open status or that a powerful interest will "take over" such funds for the express purpose of liquidating them and realizing the gain on the excess of net asset values over share prices. That would be a bonanza for our hypothetical investor who would immediately increase his investment by a third: each dollar of fund assets would appreciate from seventy-five cents to a dollar. Don't count on such a stroke of fortune, however. Most investment advisers of such funds will strongly resist the conversion to open status for fear that the funds will then suffer the same kind of redemptions by shareholders as open-end equity funds have endured in recent years. If redemptions exceed new sales, as they have in recent years in the case of most open-end equity funds, then there will be less assets to manage and the managements will have to accept either lower compensation and reduced staff or higher operating expense ratios for the funds. This spectre may compel advisers to resist the conversion of closed-end funds to open-end status, and attempts by shareholders to open up the funds generally have not been successful. Nevertheless, the possibility of a takeover bid will probably put pressure on many regular fund managements to pay regular capital distributions in addition to income dividends, and such payments are likely at least to help keep discounts from widening substantially.

How do you pick a closed-end fund? The basic thing to look for is an attractive discount and a risk level that is suited to your sleeping scale. Current discounts and premiums can be found in a weekly tabulation published in the *Wall Street Journal* on Monday, the *New York Times* on Saturday, and in several other newspapers. To gauge the attractiveness of a fund, simply compare the present discount with the historical average as I did in Table 18. Additional information about closed-end shares to help you select the fund that meets your investment objectives can be found in the Wiesenberger publication *Investment Companies.* Better yet, while you're checking, look for more than one fund for your portfolio. This would guard against the risk of buying the one fund that turned out to have the poorest record. In effect, buying a group of closed-end funds is like buying an index fund at a discount.

Can such a strategy work? It has for me. I gave my son Jonathan the royalties from *Random Walk* and invested these for him in a portfolio of closed-end funds (and dual-purpose funds, to be discussed below). During the difficult market environment from 1973 to 1979, the return from these investments was both generous and well above that for the broad market indexes, as I'll show you later. The strategy has also worked in an empirical study by Rex Thompson. Thompson showed that it was possible to make up a simple strategy of buying at a discount closed-end investment company shares that outperformed a "market" portfolio of equivalent risk. The differences in return over the period 1940 through 1975 were substantial and statistically significant.

The only real problem would occur if the discount widened in the future. In this case, the price of your shares could fall even if the value of the fund's portfolio remained the same. This latter risk is minimized, however, when you can buy the shares at discounts, as you can at this writing, that are nearly as large as they have ever been historically. These considerations do suggest, however, that closed-end shares may not always be as attractive as they are at the present time. If the discount closes (and particularly if the shares go to a premium), the shares should be sold and the proceeds invested in open-end companies or other investments.

Dual-Purpose Funds

There is another kind of closed-end fund where the risk of having the discount widen in the future is mitigated. These funds are called dual-purpose funds. A dual-purpose fund is a closed-end fund with a split personality. It consists of income (or preferred) shares and capital shares. The former receives all of the dividend and interest income produced by the assets and the latter all of the capital gains or losses produced by the fund. The beauty of the dual-purpose idea is that for every dollar invested at the start, you get two dollars worth of action.

People who like to sleep well at night tend to buy income shares, and those who are not so averse to risk taking buy the capital shares. An important consideration in buying capital shares is the leverage ratio. This is the relationship of the value of the total fund (income and capital) shares to the value of the capital shares. The higher this ratio, the greater your risk in owning these shares. But, as readers of Chapter 2 know, risk has its reward: the greater the risk, the greater the potential for making money. Since the leverage ratio is so important, it's worth taking a closer look at it.

A dual-fund operation generally starts with a leverage of two to one. This means that the fund has two dollars of total assets for each dollar the capital shareholders contribute. (The other dollar comes from the income shareowners.) For example, suppose a fund started with $20 million of assets, the capital and income shares each providing $10 million. The leverage ratio is shown in the equation below.

$$\frac{\$20 \text{ million total assets}}{\$10 \text{ million capital shares}} = \text{leverage ratio} = 2$$

The income shareowners get all the income produced by the whole $20 million of assets, and thus could reasonably expect about twice the dividend return they might get from a regular mutual fund. Similarly, if the total assets at market value went up by 10 percent from $20 million to $22 million, the entire $2 million capital gain would accrue to the capital shareholders and thus produce a percentage return of 20 percent (the $2-million gain expressed as a percentage of $10 million, the original investment). Of course, by the same logic, a 10-percent capital loss on the total portfolio would mean a 20-percent loss for the capital shareholders. It is this leverage that makes the capital shares risky and suitable only for investors able to sustain that risk.

Once the value of the fund changes from its original capital contributions, the leverage ratio will change as well. For purposes of illustration, we will say that our hypothetical fund has one very bad year, followed by two good years. In the first year, the fund loses $5 million in value; this loss is charged against those holding capital shares. The leverage ratio in the equation is now 3.

$$\frac{\$15 \text{ million total assets}}{\$5 \text{ million capital shares}} = 3$$

The next year, the fund recovers its losses, and the leverage ratio is once again 2.

$$\frac{\$20 \text{ million total assets}}{\$10 \text{ million capital shares}} = 2$$

Note that while the value of the fund increased by one-third, the value of the capital shares increased by 100 percent. Had you bought at the time the leverage ratio was 3, the value of your capital shares would have increased three times as fast as the value of the fund. You got three times the action of the fund, which is just what a leverage ratio of 3 implies.

In the third year, our fund once again does well and increases by another $5 million, an increase which goes directly to owners of the capital shares and which reduces the leverage to 1.67.

$$\frac{\$25 \text{ million total assets}}{\$15 \text{ million capital shares}} = 1.67$$

Like the shares of other closed-end investment companies, the capital shares of the dual-purpose funds have recently been selling at substantial discounts from their net asset value. The discount, coupled with the leverage feature, provides a particularly attractive investment opportunity for patient long-term investors because of another unusual feature of the dual funds.

Unlike regular closed-end investment companies, dual-purpose funds are programmed to self-destruct at a specific maturity date, during the early 1980s. On the day of reckoning, income shares are redeemed at a predetermined price, typically around the asset value when the shares were originally issued. The remaining assets belong to the capital shareholders who may, if they wish, redeem their shares at full asset value on or about the maturity date. (Alternatively, they may hold on to their shares, which will continue to be redeemable at net asset value as is the case with regular open-end funds.) Unlike the regular closed-end companies, the investor can be confident that the discount will be eliminated in the future. It is this *assured payoff at full asset value* that gives the duals their greatest edge. Thus three factors—the leverage ratio, the known redemption date, and the large discount—all combine to make the dual funds an excellent investment opportunity.

In 1979, the first dual-purpose fund matured. American Dual-Vest did in fact redeem its income shares at their predetermined value. The capital shareholders were able to redeem their shares at full net asset value. This experience gives additional confidence that there are no hidden hookers involved in this strategy.

Some attractive dual-purpose funds holding diversified portfolios and selling at discounts of about 20 percent are listed in Table 19. It shows market prices, corresponding discounts from net asset values, and leverage ratios. Remember—the higher the leverage ratio, the larger the potential return in a favorable market environment and the greater the risk in a down market.

All the funds listed above are now available at bargain-basement prices. Don't expect discounts on the duals to be above the historical average because they are all getting close to their maturity dates. Here the absolute size of the discount and the time remaining to redemption are what is important. The discounts are quite volatile and the weekly listings in the newspapers should be checked to ensure that the discounts are still large when you are about to make your investment. Remember also that the inherent leverage in these shares makes them a relatively risky investment. A leverage ratio of 2 means that the net assets of the capital shares can be expected to appreciate or depreciate twice as fast as the fund's total portfolio, which presumably will fluctuate with general market conditions. One of the most highly leveraged dual funds lost over 80 percent of its value during the bear market of the early 1970s. Similar kinds of declines occurred in the 1973–74 period.

How to Have Your Cake and Eat It Too

Suppose you like the assured disappearance of the discount provided by the closed-end funds but dislike the leverage and extra risk that goes along with buying the capital shares. Is there any way you can limit your risk and still benefit from the guaranteed appreciation implied by the elimination of the discount?

The answer is an emphatic yes. Remember that the reason the capital shares are riskier is that the income shares have a prior claim on all the company's earnings. Moreover, the investment company has to pay off the income shareholders at a predetermined price before the capital shareholders get anything. It's a very simple matter, however, to undo the leverage of the capital shares. All you do is buy one income share for every capital share you own.[3] This in effect gives you a direct share in the company's

[3]In the case of the Putnam Duo-Fund, you need buy only one-half an income share for each capital share you own. The rule for undoing leverage is to buy income and capital shares in the same ratio that the shares are outstanding.

TABLE 19
Dual-Purpose Funds

Fund	Market price (mid-1979)[a]	Discount from net asset value (mid-1979)[a]	Average discount since inception of fund	Redemption date	Leverage ratio (mid-1979)
Income and Capital	6⅞	18.9%	23%	3/31/82	2.2
Gemini[b]	16⅝	23.4	19%	12/31/84	1.4
Leverage Fund	14⅛	17.5	22%	1/1/82	1.6
Putnam Duo-Fund	9 bid	23.1	22%	1/3/83	1.9
Scudder Duo-Vest	9⅛	17.3	25%	4/1/82	1.9

[a]SOURCE: *Wall Street Journal*
[b]Managed by John Neff, the portfolio manager for the Windsor Fund. I am also a director of this fund.

assets. (If you bought all the company's income and capital shares you would own the whole portfolio directly.)

If you in fact did buy up capital and income shares in the proportions in which the shares were outstanding, it would be an easy matter to calculate the total discount of the fund. By total discount I mean the percentage by which the total market value of all the fund's shares is below the worth of the fund's assets.

Table 20 does the calculation. At the start of 1979 the securities of dual-purpose funds were selling for about eighty-five cents per dollar of the assets held by the funds. Buying up both income and capital shares is the low-risk way of ensuring that you benefit from the disappearance of the discount. Of course, you could still lose if the market went down or if your fund by chance did worse than the averages. Nevertheless, this technique is a useful one to tilt the odds of success a little more in your favor.

Jonathan's Portfolio

I mentioned that I gave my royalties from *A Random Walk Down Wall Street* to my son Jonathan. I practiced what I preached, and invested his royalties in regular and dual-purpose funds selling at substantial discounts. The investments were made mainly at the end of 1973 (near a peak in the market and thus a terrible time to invest) and near the end of 1974 (after the market had suffered a very sharp decline). Table 21 shows how Jonathan's investments have appreciated through mid-1979. Remember also that there's more guaranteed appreciation for the duals (even if the net asset value doesn't change) from the assured elimination of the discount at maturity. The strategy has outperformed the market and has been an inflation beater even during the dismal markets of the 1970s. The strategy required courage, however. The 1973 investments, made when the market was very high, were under a good deal of water at the end of 1974.[4] Fortunately, more was bought for Jonathan then when new royalty checks came in and the overall results have been more than satisfactory. The strategy has worked well for our family. It can work for yours as well.

Malkiel's Last Maxim: Don't Knock the Dow, Beat It!

The problem with the stock market today is that it's boring. Stories of overnight riches are few and far between—in contrast to gold, Chinese porcelain, art, and other exotica. It's tulip time for these other investments and, as you watch people tiptoe through them, remember that tulips are eventually buried. The stock market, on the other hand, has been buried so long that it's ready to sprout.

Why the faith in common stocks? Simple. Close examination reveals that corporate profitability and dividend yields have not

[4]According to my Rule 4 I might have switched into other closed-end funds to gain some tax advantages in 1974. However, Jonathan's tax situation did not warrant expending the brokerage charges to effect such a switch.

TABLE 20

Total Discounts for Dual-Purpose Funds (start of 1979)

Company	Price capital share	Asset value capital share	Discount capital share (%)	Price income share	Liquidation value income share	Discount income share (%)	Total net asset value	Total market value	Total discount (%)
Gemini Fund[b]	$22.25	$26.03	−14.5	$14.5	$11	31.8[a]	$60,418,000	$60,863,696	0.74[a]
Hemisphere Fund	1.375	—	—	7.375	11.44	35.5	16,400,000	12,292,061	25.05
Income and Capital Share Corp.	5.625	7.69	−26.9	10.25	10	2.5[a]	26,552,706	23,782,673	10.43
Leverage Fund of Boston	15.375	18.99	−19.0	13.625	13.725	0.7	66,000,000	57,851,664	12.35
Putnam Duo-Fund	7.5	9.70	−22.7	17.5	19.75	11.4	29,600,000	24,464,115	17.35
Scudder Duo-Vest	7.875	9.66	−18.5	8.75	9.15	4.3	108,500,000	90,171,143	16.89

[a]Premium.
[b]I am a director of this fund.

TABLE 21
Jonathan's Portfolio

	Price			Compounded rate of return including dividends and capital gains	
	Dec. 31, '73	Dec. 31, '74	June 30, '79	end 73 to mid-79	end 74 to mid-79
Regular closed-end funds					
Baker Fentress	25½ bid	15¾ bid	42½ bid	15.04%	30.72%
Dual-purpose funds					
Putnam Duo-Fund	4¼ bid	2¼ bid	9 bid	14.62%	36.08%
Scudder Duo-Vest	6⅛	3⅞	9⅛	7.52%	20.96%
Standard & Poor's Composite 500 Stock Index	97.55	68.56	102.91	5.12%	14.32%

yet been damaged—in the face of the pessimism and gloom surrounding corporate profits over the past few years. Indeed, were it not for the sharp fall in earnings multiples during the 1970s, stocks would have been an excellent inflation hedge. Because they are so low now, earnings multiples cannot fall as much as they did during the 1970s. Yet earnings and dividend growth should continue in the 1980s.

It is also well to remember the lessons of the theories we examined in Chapter 2, which suggested that capital markets are at least reasonably efficient over the long pull. Fears about the continued profitability of business investment will not be reflected in stock prices some time in the future—they are reflected in the market now. If investors perceive that the risks of investment in common stocks have increased, the financial pages will reflect that sad news very quickly and stocks will be priced, as I am sure they are today, to provide the higher future rates of return sufficient to compensate investors for the added risk.

Remember also that for the stock market as a whole Newton's law has always worked in reverse: what goes down must come back up. The Dow isn't dead—and now is a good time for you to get a running start in beating it. What I have given you in this book is a review of the major investment alternatives and a guide to how you should choose the types of securities that best suit your needs and temperament. I've also given the speculatively inclined Malkiel's rules for picking stocks and have shown how individuals and mutual funds managers have profited following these rules. I've even showed the less active among you how to beat the pros at their own game by purchasing diversified portfolios of stocks and bonds at substantial discounts below their market value. The question I leave with you now is: In five years, what will you be kicking yourself for not buying today? If you follow the advice in this book, you should be able to give yourself a big pat on the back. Good luck. And have fun.

Index